CW01375830

BONNE CHANCE

By the same author:

The Ups and Downs of Sailing, Book Guild Publishing, 2009

BONNE CHANCE

*Three Friends, Two Dogs,
and One French Manor House*

Richard Bishop

Book Guild Publishing
Sussex, England

First published in Great Britain in 2010 by
The Book Guild Ltd
Pavilion View
19 New Road
Brighton, BN1 1UF

Copyright © Richard Bishop 2010

The right of Richard Bishop to be identified as the author of this work has been asserted by him in accordance with the Copyright, Designs and Patents Act 1988.

All rights reserved. No part of this publication may be reproduced, transmitted, or stored in a retrieval system, in any form or by any means, without permission in writing from the publisher, nor be otherwise circulated in any form of binding or cover other than that in which it is published and without a similar condition being imposed on the subsequent purchaser.

Typesetting in Garamond by
Keyboard Services, Luton, Bedfordshire

Printed and bound in Thailand under the supervision of
MRM Graphics Ltd, Winslow, Bucks

A catalogue record for this book is available from
The British Library

ISBN 978 1 84624 427 8

Contents

Preface		vii
1	Nice	1
2	Le Mas Pradel	11
3	Moving	17
4	Finding Our Feet	25
5	The Work Begins	35
6	Some Risky Outings	51
7	Local Characters	59
8	Gerald and His Camper Van	71
9	Andorra la Vella	77
10	Mai	81
11	From the Sublime to the Not So Sublime	87
12	Yoko and Jacqueline	91
13	The Long Journey	95
14	Habits and Customs	99
15	The Bazalgettes and Andrew	105
16	Disaster on the Route Nationale 110	111
17	Our Paying Guests	113

18	Law and Order	119
19	Local People and Local History	125
20	Mind Your Language	131
21	Filming with Mai	137
22	The Festival Season	141
23	Winter Weather	147
24	A Walk in the Garrigue	151
25	Montpellier Airport	153
26	More Friends	157
27	It's The All My Fault Club	165
28	Antiques and Sales	167
29	Storm Clouds	173
30	Our Future	177

Preface

Let me introduce us – the three friends, also known as 'The Team'. Alan Greene was the eldest member of 'The Team'. He served as a captain in the Royal Engineers during the Second World War. He was assistant manager of a tea plantation prior to his call-up, where he was spoilt by his eleven servants. After the war he was a consultant engineer to a chemical company. After many years of service his world suddenly changed when he entered a chemical vessel to check it after

Alan and Faye with Jasper and Katie

a breakdown. Tragically chemicals remained inside it, and this caused chest and brain damage.

Alan's wife Faye returned to her profession as a nurse, caring for mentally disturbed patients and general nursing to earn her living. Faye's wide experience in health care was appreciated by everyone she helped, both inside her profession and in her good works for those in trouble which occupied much of her life. She helped me recover from my life-changing event of divorcing my wayward wife, and my brief nervous breakdown.

My own career in teaching as Head of Department, Principal of Further Education had been a rewarding experience, but working in dusty surroundings in workshops was the cause of my asthma and bronchitis, and the onset of arthritis was the last straw, which made me apply to retire on health grounds.

Returning home from our Spanish holiday by car one year proved to be a nightmare. By the time we had reached the border the combined total of our ready cash had dwindled alarmingly. We soon

Alan, Faye and Richard walking in the Cevennes

discovered that the French banks were all closed, and even the shopkeepers had closed their shutters for the national holiday.

We were obliged to press on towards Roscoff, because we both were due to start work in a few days' time, and our cash would soon run out, leaving the petrol tank and our stomachs empty. Our first lucky break was finding a family run guesthouse off the beaten track, where we were treated very generously considering the modest charges. We still had enough money to fill the petrol tank, but not enough to fill our stomachs. We finally reached Treboul in Brittany before the tank was almost empty, and we had run out of steam.

Our second lucky break of the journey was finding accommodation with Odette, and our charming hostess was prepared to wait until the banks opened before we settled our bill. Odette soon discovered that Faye and I were keen sailors, so she thoughtfully introduced us to the local sailing club where we enjoyed the friendly atmosphere, and the Kir which is liqueur blackcurrant juice, mixed with fine quality white wine.

One of the club's visitors seemed to be very taken with us, and seemed to be weighing us up. Eventually he asked us if we would

Le Mas Pradel with the author at the front door of our four storey French manor house

consider exchanging houses for a month the following summer. We agreed to swap our Cornish creekside cottage for his apartment in the village of Falicon on the outskirts of Nice.

Faye and I invited two of our neighbours to spend a five-week holiday travelling across France and four of the weeks spent in Nice. It was a superb opportunity to get to know the Alpes-Maritime, the Riviera, and parts of the nearby coast of Italy. Naturally we fell in love with this part of France, and the idea of settling there became planted in my mind.

1

Nice

The Pink Panther

Our holiday apartment in the village of Falicon was beginning to heat up in the early morning sunshine, and my three friends and I agreed to spend the day visiting the flower market in Nice which was well over a thousand feet below us. A leisurely lunch in the nearby popular restaurant with its customers packed in like sardines had a superb ambience and first class food, so with the prospect of cooling off in the sea afterwards, our day was going to be perfect.

Unfortunately we all needed to cash our traveller's cheques, before we could relax and enjoy ourselves. We soon found a bank which was staffed by cashiers wearing shorts and t-shirts, and their workstations were scattered about in a very informal manner. We joined a queue which moved at a snail's pace towards a cashier who was dispensing cash as though he was giving his own money away.

Directly in front of me four foreign-looking men chatted to one another in a language which sounded Eastern Mediterranean, so I was astounded to see them offer Irish passports to the cashiers to verify their identities, before receiving their cash. Each of them had a pallor which was not in keeping with the summer sunshine, rather I thought they had been deprived of sunshine for a long time as prisoners, or perhaps as patients in hospital.

It did cross my mind that they were going to hold up the bank, and in my fertile mind I even considered what I would do if they produced their guns. However, I decided that although I did not like the looks of them, they most probably were perfectly normal and quite harmless. My friends who had been standing behind me in the queue did not seem concerned about these men, so I decided that perhaps there was perfect reasonable explanation for their presence.

After our delightful meal and a wander though the flower market we settled down to a pleasant afternoon on the beach, but all too soon the late afternoon news vendors arrived. I bought a copy of the late edition for us to read after our evening meal. However, I was astounded to see that the headlines gave the dynamic news that terrorists had created chaos in Paris with their bombs, leaving many dead and injured. Four photos accompanied the headlines.

I recognised three of the photos as being the men from the bank. Unfortunately I did not get a clear view of the fourth man. It was obviously my duty to contact the police and give my witness, which I considered would help trace the terrorists.

When I arrived at the local police station, the policeman on duty was at a complete loss as what to do with me, but eventually his superior telephoned the Sûreté. I was then bundled into the back of a police car, the doors were locked, and I was driven across town at high speed with the siren blaring. By this time I wondered whether I was being treated as a prisoner rather than a helpful witness.

We soon arrived at the very impressive headquarters of the Regional Securété. I was then escorted to a dismal room on the second floor, which reminded me of an old-fashioned classroom with its high pedestal teacher's desk, and rows of wooden tables and chairs. The entire building seemed to be devoid of staff except for my interrogator, who reminded me of Peter Sellers when he played the part of Inspector Clouseau in the film *The Pink Panther*.

I explained as best I could how I came to identify the men in the bank as the terrorists who were being sought throughout France. I also tried to explain how important it was to contact the bank to trace their passports, as these would show what bogus identities they were using.

Clouseau laboriously tried to complete my witness statement without success, and each failure ended in shreds in his waste bin. The more frustrated he became the more he resembled Peter Sellers, and I began to find it difficult not to laugh at his discomfort. However, I was brought back to earth when he informed me that 'Le Patron' had returned to his penthouse suite and he had been ordered to escort me there for further questioning.

The first thing I did was to ask 'Le Patron' for an English interpreter to assist me, but he said that my French was better than his English, and he was sure that we could manage. His priority was to check my identity. This was impossible because my passport and driving licence were in my car, which was in an underground car park some considerable distance away, and all I had was my purse.

I was once again dispatched in haste in one of their cars with the siren blaring, just to collect my car. Parking in the city centre is almost impossible so he authorised me to use his private parking space. Alas! A gendarme was guarding it when I arrived, and he told me to get lost. Nobody in their right mind would dare argue with these ferocious characters. However, I plucked up courage and told him that Le Patron would be exceedingly angry if he delayed me. I thought for a moment that he was going to have a fit, because his face had become a deep shade of purple and I did not like the way he was fondling his revolver.

Back in the penthouse I was reassured that I was not a lunatic, and Le Patron telephoned the Sûreté in Paris with the news that the terrorists had been seen in Nice. To my pleasant surprise coffee and biscuits were served, and he thanked me for my help and said that it was such a pity that the French were not as co-operative as I had been.

Next morning 'Terrorists Seen in Monaco' was the newspaper headline. I not only identified them, but I had been standing right next to them for at least ten minutes!

My lasting memory of the day's events was not that I had been so close to four murderers, but the surreal feeling that I had been on a film set with Peter Sellers acting the part of Insector Clouseau.

Vertigo

The village of Falicon was an excellent base on a mountain close to Nice, where my three friends and I were spending our four week-summer holiday. We all took it in turn to select the activity of the day, although we tried to reserve alternate days for pottering about, and relaxing on the public beaches.

BONNE CHANCE

Jack, Elsie, Alan and the photographer waiting for their ice cold drinks

The mountains fall down into the Mediterranean

The three of us and our new yacht; only joking of course!

When it was my turn I chose to adventure on minor roads for the excitement of driving, finding unspoilt parts, avoiding the flocks of tourists, and the enjoyment of soaking up the beauty of the Alpes-Maritimes.

My first adventure was to cross a mountain range where tree felling was taking place. The long hard slog up the torturous narrow road, devoid of barriers, past increasingly long drops, with hardly any space to pass other vehicles, began to make me increasingly uneasy the further up the mountain we climbed.

Suddenly I heard a huge tree transporter coming thundering down the road towards us. It was laden with massive tree trunks, and was travelling at a frightening speed. I could not see that it would be able to stop, nor was there enough room for it to pass us.

I spotted a slightly wider section of the road a couple of hundred yards ahead, so I accelerated towards it, and parked with our wheels almost hanging over the edge of the road with a drop of many hundreds of feet for us to fall if I misjudged my parking. The driver of the transporter made no attempt to stop, and his monstrous vehicle shook our car, avoiding us by inches, and shattering my self-confidence. When we reached the top of the mountain I was surprised to find the road flattened out for a several kilometres, and suddenly ahead was nothing but glorious deep blue sky.

As we approached the void, a notice informed us of the danger of twenty-eight *virages* (bends) ahead. The sensation of toppling over the edge and seeing the fantastic panorama of the Alpes-Maritimes stretching as far as the eyes could see was a memorable moment. Another notice with an arrow pointed to a gap in the stone wall at the edge of the road, where some poor soul had disappeared through it to oblivion. Lovers Leap was the name on the noticeboard.

I had to reverse back up several of the bends which had no security

Monte Carlo seafront and beach

barriers. One of the most difficult proved almost impossible to negotiate as the handbrake was unable to hold the car on the incredibly steep bend. Alan offered to take over the driving, because he could see I was losing my nerve. It was a come-down, having competed in three national car rallies. However, it spurred me on to complete fourteen more of these *virages* before we reached the bottom of the flight, and some of these were just as difficult. What I did not realise was that there was a smaller range of mountains to cross before we could head back to Nice.

Anyone reading about this trip would think that I would have steered clear of driving on minor roads in the Alpes-Maritimes. However, the call of the challenge was too great, and at the first opportunity we went back for some more punishment.

The route I chose followed along the side of a spectacular gorge at well over a thousand feet above a river below. The road we followed was a minor one with a stunning view of a near vertical mountainside of considerable elevation. What appeared to be a small ledge ran horizontally, about level with us. The further we drove, the less I could work out where our chosen scenic route could possibly lead to. Too late to turn back because the road was too narrow to turn around in, so I decided to press ahead, and gradually the road began to turn towards the ledge on the other side. We were now driving along a single-track road without any barriers to stop us falling a thousand feet if I slipped over the edge.

Jack began to have a panic attack of vertigo, so I foolishly decided to stop at a beauty spot, which turned out to be called 'The Soldiers Leap'. The poor soul had plenty of time to regret his decision, likewise I regretted my choice of parking for the passengers to enjoy the view. Jack was petrified when he peered over the edge, and we both had a bad turn of vertigo. I continued driving with my heart in my mouth with Jack expecting me to drive off the road at any moment. Needless to say Jack declined to return to the mountains.

The next excuse for driving in the mountains was to visit the ski slopes, and I took the opportunity to follow a small road which led towards the high mountain peaks where I hoped to watch the mountaineers rock climbing. I had been a keen climber myself, and I expected to see some more advanced rock climbing than I had ever aspired to.

As we drove higher and higher towards the rocky mountain tops, we saw a warning sign that there had been a landslide and the road was closed. The four of us set off on foot, with the intention of finding a good view point. Bulldozers had made a rough track over the massive pile of debris, which was only fit for pedestrians.

As we approached the landslide I was amazed to hear the whine of a small car approaching us at high speed from the far side of the rough track! It was a *deux chevaux* with two nuns in it who were oblivious of their danger, but enjoying the thrill of the downhill run. The car bounced and wobbled as it traversed the landslip debris, and continued onwards as though they were racing in the Monte Carlo Rally. How they managed to negotiate the bends I do not know. It transpired that the nuns made regular trips to and from their mountain retreat. It must have been a miracle that they had survived their reckless driving. Alan's comment was, 'God certainly looks after his own.'

I seemed to make a habit of driving in stressful situations.

Death in the Spanish mountains

Faye and I had spent a summer holiday touring France and Spain, staying in all sorts of modest accommodation, and for a whole week we were obliged to stay in a commercial hotel in an industrial town near Tarragona in Spain. It lacked any air conditioning and the only way we could converse was for me to speak to the manager in French. We enjoyed our stay, in spite of having a Secret Service agent keeping us under surveillance.

On our way back home we decided to take a scenic route, and stop over in a small town called Ainsa, which was well placed for us to visit the Parque Nacional de Ordesa. I estimated that we could follow a single-track road, the N260, and drive into the park, following the Rio Ara.

The further we went, the more the route became unbelievably hair-raising. For starters we had to drive across a timber-framed bridge spanning a deep gully, which only had timber kerbs to stop anyone falling into the gully. Shortly afterwards the road consisted of a narrow ledge which had been blasted out of the face of the mountain. The road surface was loose gravel, and there were no barriers at all to stop vehicles falling into the valley some thousand feet below. Each blind bend in the track had a warning sign painted on the rock, which indicated that everyone should sound their horn, as violent braking could cause vehicles to slide off the track into oblivion.

Eventually we left the ledge, the valley opened up, and Monte Perdido which is about ten thousand feet high could be seen ahead. Below us an ancient iron bridge spanned the river, and a small cluster of stone houses close by made an interesting spot for us to visit, so we drove down to the bridge. However, we found a noticeboard which declared that the bridge had been condemned many decades ago, and the planks were all loose and several were missing. I considered that it was unsafe for pedestrians and Faye said that poisonous snakes were in the river. I plucked up courage and crossed the bridge, expecting to fall through one of the gaps any moment. Faye must have been pulling my leg about the water snakes because she waded across, coming out looking refreshed after our long journey.

On our way back along the narrow ledge I regained some of my confidence in coping with my fear of heights, when suddenly a Land Rover filled with Germans started to harass us by driving closer and closer to our back bumper, sounding their hooter and jeering at us all the time. I concluded that they had seen our GB badge and had decided to settle a score with us for winning the Second World War. Their driving was so aggressive I made a dash to a wider section of the track, which I remembered was round the next bend. We parked safely and let the Germans pass us shouting abuse. In my mind my worst fears were confirmed, that they would have been delighted if we had been forced off the track to take the short cut into the river a thousand feet below.

On our arrival at Ainsa a very kind gentleman helped us find accommodation in the only spare bedroom in the town's only hotel, and that was in the attic. The next morning we learned that a dreadful accident had occurred when a Land Rover full of German climbers drove off a local mountain road to their deaths.

2

Le Mas Pradel

The persistent winter rains soon dilute the West Country's charms, and the dark skies make even the most cheerful folk depressed. It was no wonder the newspapers are half filled with holiday adverts and 'Properties for sale abroad'. My best friends Faye and Alan and I were enjoying the comfort of a log fire in my creekside cottage, as it was being buffeted by a winter storm, when our conversation turned towards the possibility of moving somewhere warmer and drier. It was not long before we began to seriously consider moving abroad.

Alan had lived in India for ten years, and he yearned to return to a hot climate. Spain was his first choice because he had been brought up in the Argentine and spoke Spanish fluently. Faye's love was the Scottish Borders, and she had lived near Edinburgh which is a fabulous

Alan and Faye walking along the famous 'Promenade des Anglais'

city, so she preferred to return to her roots. The only problem was the east coast weather is very cold, so that choice was a non-starter.

My own choice was the south of France, for its super climate and of course the fabulous countryside. Faye and I had sailed from the Channel Isles all the way to Spain and made a good many friends en route, and we found the French to be helpful and polite. Alan, Faye and I had fallen in love with the south of France when we had spent that long holiday in Nice. We finally agreed that it would be a good compromise, and at least my French was good enough for us to get by until we could pick up the language.

We all three made up our minds to return to France and find a suitable property for renovation, which could be used as accommodation for guests and members of our families.

Some months later Faye found an interesting advert for a detached period property in the south of France, to rent for only thirty pounds per week for prospective buyers. The modest asking price and the cheap rental, together with the situation in one of the Departments which have an interesting coastline, were too good to be true. Faye went ahead and telephoned the owner to find out more about her property. We booked our holiday with a view to purchasing 'Les Volets Rouge'. Failing that we would spend our holiday looking for our dream house elsewhere.

Alan, his sister Judy, Faye and I packed our bags and set off on our adventure, with a thousand or more kilometres drive to Les Volets Rouge. We were hoping to find a large property, suitable for Faye, Alan and I to restore with a view to spending the remainder of our retirement years in France. We were naturally looking forward to seeing the place and meeting its English vendor.

Unfortunately our first glance at the situation of the property confirmed that, with no parking facilities, and a back garden which needed crampons instead of wellies because it was just a slice of mountainside, we could not even consider anything so inconvenient. The good news was we could stay as long we wished, and we had found a good base for our search for our ideal home. The bad news was finding scorpions had set up home in our holiday let and resented our intrusion. They also did not take kindly to our attempts to evict them from our shoes, bedding and other comfortable nooks and crannies. When Judy first saw these black beasts on her bedroom wall she mistook them for ornaments.

We decided to visit Nice hoping to find something suitable at a price we could afford, but the only attractive properties we could find were new detached suburban houses which certainly did not tick all the boxes for us. However our trip served a good purpose because we realised that we stood a better chance of finding what we wanted in the area nearer Les Volets Rouge, where affordable larger properties were available at prices we could afford. Day after day we scoured the area where we were staying without any success, and with only one more day left for house hunting our prospects looked very hopeless. A small market town not far away had been overlooked, so we decided to try the two estate agents there first thing in the morning.

To our delight the first agent said that he might have two properties which could suit our needs. Unfortunately the most promising one, which was actually in the town, had not been put on the books, so it was not possible to view the interior. However the agent realised that we were interested in the property, so he decided to drive us to the ancient Mas hoping that he would find the owner at home.

Just one look down the private road leading directly to the huge building, with its own old stone bridge, was all that it took to make

1983 our new home, Le Mas Pradel

our hearts start thumping with anticipation of finding what was inside: our future home!

This fine old building was full of promise, but it was obviously in a very bad state, and it would need a great commitment of our time, effort, and a lot of our hard-earned savings to make it habitable.

Lillian, the daughter-in-law of the owner, lived in the converted cow shed, which had belonged to the estate at one time. Suddenly she appeared running down the lane towards us carrying the largest front door key I had ever seen. She quickly introduced herself and

Our derelict Mas (Manor House)

asked if we would like to see over the house. Naturally we agreed that we would be delighted to follow her. She hurriedly threw back the shutters one by one as we went from floor to floor, and room to room. The high granite stairs leading to the pigeon loft were tiring but nevertheless very impressive, and the size of each room was considerable compared to what we were used to. At this stage we were very impressed with the potential of this great building, and its situation was ideal. However the building was in desperate need of lots of TLC, and some major repairs.

Fortunately the French are very loath to undertake renovations of large old houses, because it is so much cheaper to buy new-build or modern houses. Building your own has become the most popular trend. With only twenty-four hours left before we planned to return home, it was essential to survey the property and decide if we could afford to undertake the renovations, and what work we could do ourselves. We would also need to make a formal offer if we three could all agree that we had found our ideal project for our retirement years.

Our last day at Les Volets Rouge was indeed hectic. Completion of the formal offer was our first priority. The repairs and rendering of the façade had to be negotiated with a reputable builder, and the installation of a telephone had to be ordered because it usually took months before it was completed. We discovered from our visit to the notaire that we had committed ourselves to purchasing a Mas, which is the nearest equivalent to a manor house, a very long driveway with its Roman bridge, a well, one chicken house, enough land to keep us busy, and a small car park. We had in effect bought the residue of an estate which included the hamlet of Perriere where the farm workers lived.

It was all very well signing the provisional contract of intent, but back in England we had a substantial list of problems to deal with before we could move into our new home. Back in 1983–4 it was difficult to get a visa to reside permanently in France, unless we had an adequate income and savings, enough to ensure that we would not be a burden on the state. We also had to satisfy various authorities that we were desirable persons with no criminal records and not suffering from any mental illness. Some six months or so later our passports were returned with our visas granting us our residency for life.

Faye and Alan sold their Plymouth town house, and their Cornish cottage, and then moved into my creekside Cornish cottage, together with their furniture and effects, which they stored in my old coach house.

All our eggs were now in one basket in readiness for the sale of my property, which took longer than anticipated. We had been given a final date for us to take up our residency by the French Consulate, and it was going to be touch and go to make the deadline.

The only other important item in our list of things to do was to attend French classes, but we had been so busy we had hardly any time to relax. I strongly recommend anyone wishing to emigrate to a foreign country to have at least some grasp of their new language before they start their new life. We had to cope with my French for a while!

3

Moving

Departure

Pickfords' largest continental removal van eased its way along our narrow waterfront lane to my cottage, in preparation for loading all our prized possessions which we were taking to France. Twelve hours later the removal lads had squeezed every item into their capacious vehicle, with the exception of a very heavy garden roller which was abandoned to rust away quietly in the orchard.

The next morning our worldly possessions left Forder in the tender care of Patrick the driver, who had planned to arrive at Saint Ambroix a day later than ourselves. Alan, Faye and their two dogs Candy and Jasper, and myself squeezed into my large Fiat, surrounded by a mountain of 'must have' items, which had been pushed into every nook and cranny.

Our goodbye party for our neighbours and friends, and all our farewells to members of both our families had already concluded our lives in the West Country, so we set off on our long journey to the south of France. Although I was relieved to be on the move I was sure that we all were apprehensive about how our new lives would pan out.

Throughout our long journey I had plenty of time to come to terms with my feelings about leaving my friends and family, especially my mother who would be the most upset at my leaving. I determined to return twice a year to stay with her, and to telephone home regularly. Poor Mother had taken one look at a photo of our new home and said, 'But it looks like a glue factory.' She obviously was not impressed with me leaving The Moorings at Forder.

Frequent stops to feed and water the dogs, and not forgetting the two-legged passengers' needs, slowed our progress southwards. An overnight stay in a motel refreshed our enthusiasm for our new country with its varied scenery and vast tracts of uninhabited space.

Driving on the right-hand side of the road had already become second nature to me, although the front seat passengers were often taken to be the driver. Many a French person was shocked to see Faye apparently doing her make up while negotiating roundabouts in a hands-free mode. On one occasion I turned sharply across the road and into the forecourt of a garage when Faye was reading a newspaper in the front passenger seat. The poor woman who was seated on a chair waiting for her clients threw her hands in the air in despair, fearing that some lunatic female was about to squash her flat against the garage wall. She dived for cover and barely regained her composure and then started to laugh when she realised her mistake.

The last part of our journey took us through the Ardeche mountains, and as the scenery began to unfold as we descended towards our destination, it dawned on me that we were passing through our new home patch. Faye, Alan and I began to be excited at the prospect of reaching Saint Ambroix and Le Mas Pradel. The dogs began to stir and half-heartedly wag their tails, but as we drew into the town square their tails wagged enthusiastically.

Our very first priority was to visit our new home to make sure that it was still standing. Of course it was, and two of its façades had been rendered in our long absence, giving the huge building a new air of self importance, after decades of neglect.

Unfortunately we had not completed our purchase and we needed to withdraw a substantial amount of francs, which were to be 'paid under the table'. However the Credit Agricole had insufficient funds. The bank manager was very embarrassed, and asked us to drive to Alès and collect our cash from the main branch of his bank. We spent several hours walking about with our cash in a supermarket carrier bag hidden beneath some shopping, whilst waiting for our appointment with the house agent and the two vendors at the house agent's office. The completion went ahead without any misunderstandings, until it came to the division of the 'under the table cash' which was being split between the owner of the house and the owner of the additional land which we had negotiated. Neither party could agree, until the agent produced his cigarette lighter, and threatened to set light to the bundle of notes if they could not agree. In less than no time at all the problem was resolved and we received the huge front door key to the Mas.

The traditional way to celebrate the sale of a property is for the agent and his wife to invite everybody concerned to the agent's favourite bar in town, for a drink or two to seal the sale. During the impromptu party I heard the agent ask 'the French group' how we could possibly fit into Saint Amboisien society. After much laughter and suggestions as to which club or society might be suitable for us, they gave up trying. It was finally agreed that Le Mas Pradel and its owners would certainly be the centre of notoriety. Those predictions turned out to be so very true.

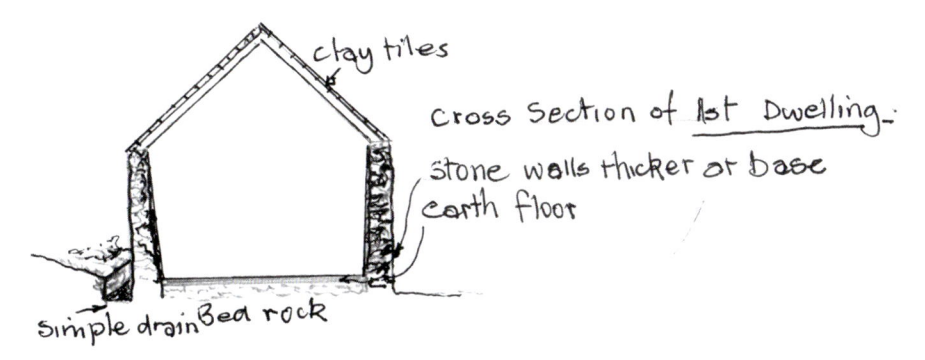

Cross section of 1st dwelling

Rear view of Mas Pradel

Moving in and our survey

A long time before Faye had ever considered moving abroad, she had her fortune read by a well renowned palmist. He predicted that she would live abroad in a long white house, where the leaves were falling at the wrong time of the year and there was something strange about the door key. These predictions and more personal ones came true.

In our absence the builders had made a good job of re-rendering the two main façades, but in the process they had covered the entire building in a thick layer of dust and debris. They had also left the shutters and windows on the third floor open for several months, causing them all to bang to and fro and break every pane of glass. We also discovered that the roof leaked in twenty-eight places. The good news was that it seldom rained in Saint Ambroix, the bad new was that it rains very hard when it does. To make matters worse our builder was not free to re-roof the house until mid winter!

There was a remarkable absence of any form of sanitation in the house. The outside earth closet had fallen apart decades ago, and it was on the wrong side of our boundary. We retired to the Hotel Moderne where we had been staying, and considered the likelihood of the three of us making Le Mas habitable. One thing was absolutely certain and that was going to be the installation of a modern sanitation system. The restoration would have to wait.

Patrick the Pickfords' driver attempted to negotiate the narrow bridge which crossed a small river leading to the property, unfortunately his vehicle nearly got stuck! One of the neighbours suggested that we should knock the ornamental pillar down to make more room. Alas even that would not allow the van to get access to the house. One of the onlookers stepped forward and offered to resolve our problem by hiring a delivery van for us, so that I could run a relay service collecting the furniture from the removal van which was then parked in the market square. The two casual labourers who had been hired for the day to help with the unloading would then be able to follow Faye's instructions as to where they should move each item. Patrick and I loaded the delivery van countless times and I returned with our effects.

I was curious to find each time I returned to the market place that a local priest remained watching Patrick and me loading our furniture and effects into the delivery van, with more than a passing interest. Perhaps he was hoping to find that the new arrivals were wealthy Catholics who would contribute to the church coffers.

The two casual labourers were as different as chalk and cheese. One was middle aged, rotund and out of condition, the other was a 'twiggy-like' youngster who was clearly not used to lifting anything heavier than a sausage roll. It was a strange sight seeing Faye directing them with sign language and Frenglish, as they staggered up the flights of tall granite steps towards the upper floors with wardrobes filled with clothes. As the day moved on our hard-working labourers became more and more down at heel, due to the weight of all the heavy furniture which seemed to endlessly arrive in my van. The poor souls began to insist their contract ended at five pm when they were due to be back at Bagnols, where Patrick had collected them. The only realistic chance of completing the move, was for me to give

The front door

them a lift home as late as possible. In the meantime Faye and Alan had been working their socks off cleaning and arranging the numerous rooms with our furniture, making our Mas look quite homely.

Throughout the day I had been adrenaline fuelled and I was in the mood to remind myself what it was like competing in motor sport. I maintained a very high speed whilst the older labourer sat next to me transfixed by the speedometer, which he thought was recording kilometres per hour. He was also frightened at sitting on the wrong side of the car. He remained drenched in sweat whilst the youngster kept his eyes closed until we reached our destination. My hapless passengers were so relieved that they had survived their Monte Carlo Rally experience without any mishaps. However, I thoroughly enjoyed the drive home which was even faster. I resolved that in future I would drive at a more moderate pace.

On my return to the fold I found that Patrick had declined to spend the night alone in such a spooky place. However he accepted Faye's invitation to join us for a meal at the Hotel Moderne to celebrate our successful move. When asked what he thought about our new town, he said he would like to put windows in his van, park it in the market place, and take up permanent residence, During the meal he spent his time trying to chat up the attractive waitress, thinking that she would not understand his cheeky remarks. That was not the case! She enjoyed his banter but declined his kind offer to drive her home in his huge van. It was to be our last night at the hotel so we made the most of the bathroom and toilet facilities, because the only facility we had at the Mas was one solitary cold water tap.

Our number one priority was to install a WC and downstairs cloakroom, because we had been obliged to go back to nature using plastic buckets instead of flush toilets which everyone else used in France. The summer heat had baked the earth so hard it was like concrete, which made it impossible to bury the contents of the buckets, so we resorted to filling rabbit holes if we were lucky enough to find an empty one. This routine continued for several weeks while we waited impatiently for our contractor to install a modern cesspit sewerage system.

One day before the installation a lady friend called to see Faye. I politely invited her to step inside an unoccupied downstairs room, for a chat with Faye. Alas! As I started to push the very large and heavy door open, I realised that Faye must be answering the call of nature, seated on her bucket just inside the door, and I was pushing her out of sight! I quickly redirected our visitor to the kitchen where the aroma of percolated coffee was more inviting.

We were well and truly relieved when the contractor installed our new sewerage system. We opted not to have the usual ribbon-cutting ceremony to declare the new cloakroom open, and instead let Faye mark the event by flushing the toilet.

4

Finding Our Feet

Fences and Boundaries

Not long after we had settled down to our new lives working hard restoring our new home, we decided to take a break and spend some quality time on our large first floor terrace which overlooks Saint Ambroix. The balmy night air with the aroma of wild herbs, and a bottle of local red wine, lulled us into a state of contentment and satisfaction with our purchase of our Mas. It was well past one o'clock when I noticed a light moving about in the abandoned vineyard which was adjacent to our house and the terrace. The torchlight was now moving towards our rear garden, it was moving erratically and it was illuminating a man's face.

'I suggested that I went to investigate, but neither Alan or Faye thought it was a wise move. Nevertheless, I ran down the steps and along the front of the house to head off the intruder who was obviously going towards the other end of the house.

I was confronted by the man standing at the top of a steep grassy slope. He was staring at me and holding large picture of Christ, which he illuminated with his torch, and at the same time it showed his contorted expression. I challenged him to explain what he was doing on our land so late at night. His response was to run down the slope directly at me, and then stop about ten feet in front of me. He remained silent. I dismissed the nutter with a few sharp comments, and indicated that he should get lost, then started to walk casually back to the terrace.

The sound of footsteps running towards me made me change tactics, and I ran hell for leather along the courtyard and up the stairs to the terrace door, which was promptly shut in my face. Fortunately it was reopened!

Our policeman neighbour Daniel answered my telephone call for help, and told me to meet him at our front door. He arrived within a few minutes armed with his truncheon and torch. I was then asked to explain what had happened, before he set off tracking the route the intruder had taken, while I followed on behind. As soon as Daniel had recognised the house the track led to he told me to stay put whilst he dealt with the problem.

The residents of the house were an elderly father and his son who had become deranged by over studying at university. As Daniel approached the house I could hear an almighty row going on inside. I waited for a quarter of an hour before Daniel returned to reassure me that the intruder would not be causing any more trouble, as he had forbidden him to enter our property again. Having thanked our saviour for his rude awakening from his night's sleep, I walked back to the welcome lights of the Mas. It crossed my mind that proper fencing might have prevented the unpleasant incident. I wondered what Alan, Faye and the two dogs would think about being fenced in.

Jasper and Candy had been accustomed to visiting two charming old ladies each morning when they were staying at my creekside cottage during the run-up to our move to France. The neighbours took a fancy to the dogs and rewarded them with tasty tit-bits. Both dogs loved their freedom of the riverside at Forder and decided to cultivate some new friends in the nearby houses in Saint Ambroix. It was several years before one of their benefactors 'told tales' about their activities, and said how much they enjoyed the rituals of Jasper's and Candy's morning visits. No wonder our crafty dogs had such poor appetites each morning.

The thought of enclosing our property would have sent the wrong message to the neighbours and the local residents, that we did not wish to be included in the community. Jasper and Candy would have been appalled at the loss of their freedom and the joy of roaming the glorious countryside was the big event of the day for us all, especially the dogs.

I remember asking the mayor of one of the local small communities, which had attracted a good many foreign newcomers, what effect the influx of new residents was having on his community. He said quite emphatically that there were far too many newcomers, and their enclosed houses were eroding the very things which attracted them in the first place. The French way of life was also being adversely effected.

We had chosen very wisely because our household was the only one in the town to have only English residents.

Captain Charles Rousseau and the Resistance Movement

Our holiday at Les Volets Rouge enabled us to find our dream property. It also was instrumental in us meeting Charles and his wife, and making our enduring friendship. The locals said of Charles that he was more British than the British, and suggested that we would be interested in his work as an undercover intelligence agent throughout

Captain Charles Rousseau

the Second World War. His wife called him Papillon (butterfly) because he flitted from one branch of the Resistance to another.

His chosen name was Jean Barre, which stood him in good stead because someone denounced him to the SS by saying that Charles was Jean Barre. Fortunately the French police ridiculed this information, because Jean Barre was a well-known historical seafaring captain who had been the scourge of the British Navy for many years. He escaped being executed by a gnats's whisker.

Captain Rousseau of the Lincoln Regiment, was our friend's honorary rank, and was in charge of the resistance movement in the Le Havre region. I always enjoyed listening to Captain Alan Greene of the Royal Engineers and Captain Charles of the Lincoln Regiment taking about their war service. I was enthralled listening to their tales of dangerous activities.

Some time prior to the invasion Charles was ordered to find out what was hidden inside a blockhouse, which was situated some miles inland from the Port of Le Havre. Charles's men were unable to discover what was inside, because the place was heavily guarded. They did manage to estimate that the only way to destroy the block house, was to drop a bomb directly onto the steel door. After the war had ended Charles was returning to the UK in an RAF aircraft sitting in the jump seat chatting to the pilot. It transpired that the pilot had dropped the bomb which destroyed the block house and its contents.

When our forces advanced on Le Havre they were surprised to find very little resistance. This was due entirely to the destruction of the communication centre, which had been inside the block house. The German forces could no longer co-ordinate the defence of the massive and numerous gun emplacements. Thousands of lives of the allied forces were saved as a direct result of one bomb on the communication bunker, but it was the resistance men who provided intelligence for the RAF's air strike.

One day a dirty-looking man was found by his men, wandering aimlessly, and talking in a strange language. None of the team could make out what he was about, so they took him to be interrogated by Charles, in case the man was being planted to infiltrate the unit. If that was the case, the man would be shot. Fortunately Charles managed to fathom what had occurred to this unfortunate soul.

Ivan had been in a team of Russian forced labourers constructing gun emplacements, and their conditions were unbelievably harsh. One weekend the German officers were called away to a conference, so the Russians decided to go on strike because they were starving to death. Alas! When the officers returned they ordered their soldiers to put all of the Russians into a giant concrete mixer which was then left running long enough to kill its occupants. Finally the mixer was emptied of the bodies, and the soldiers returned to their sleeping quarters. Some time during the night Ivan recovered consciousness and found that he was underneath the pile of his compatriots' bodies. He crawled away to safety and wandered about, threatening to cut his wrist with a razor blade.

Prior to the Allies' invasion, Charles had been instructed to visit all the mayors in his patch, to pass on the orders for the Resistance to follow when the Allied troops approached, so that their efforts could be co-ordinated to have the maximum effect. He was standing in a village square talking to one of the mayors when suddenly a rifle shot rang out, and an SS officer dropped dead at his feet, still holding his revolver with which he was going to shoot him. Ivan, who had spent the remainder of the war working with the resistance cell, had been acting as a body guard for Charles. He spotted the officer who had drawn his revolver so he shot him.

Each time we were invited to their home for afternoon tea, the table was laid out with cakes and goodies, although we suspected that they could ill afford their generosity.

During one of my holidays in Le Havre in 1947, my penfriend took me on an illegal tour of the German defence system which stretched all along the eastern coast. My friend Michael warned me that it might be dangerous where we were going, so we had to be on the look out for booby traps and explosives. We wandered through gun emplacements, access tunnels and observation posts and fortunately did not come across anything dangerous.

The pièce de résistance was the complex which had been intended to house the world's largest gun which had been due to shell Southampton. The shells were housed beneath a small hill and a railway system carried them directly to lifts which raised them up to the loading platform. The gun turret itself was huge, but the armoured plated roof had to be removed during the installation of the gun itself. Members of the local Resistance kept the RAF up to date on the constructional progress. A single bomber was dispatched the day of the installation and scored a direct hit inside the turret, putting the gun out of action for the remainder of the war. Once again the brave men of the Resistance had put their lives on the line, keeping watch on the German activities.

A very poignant event which occurred not far from the MAS was related by a good neighbour to illustrate just one of the tragedies that happened during the occupation. The ordinary German foot soldiers were regarded by the locals as ordinary men who had been dragged into the conflict against their wishes. However the officers and SS members were detested not only by the French but also by the ordinary German soldiers.

The Germans had taken three hostages in a reprisal for the activities of the local Resistance in the Saint Ambroix area. They were of course executed. The members of the local Resistance decided to take their own revenge by taking three of the German soldiers, who were made to face a firing squad as their punishment. One of these poor souls pleaded to have a last request, which was for him to hold the photo of his girlfriend which he carried in his wallet. His wish was granted but, instead of holding the photo, he put it into his mouth and ate it, before he and the other two were executed.

The sad conclusion to my story of Charles and his wife was that they died not long after each other. They had requested that Alan, Faye and I should lead the cortège to the local cemetery in front of their only son Ivan, who had lost the respect of his parents.

Guests behind bars

The reason we purchased our dilapidated Mas was to restore it with a view to converting it into a private hotel and creating a two double bedroom gite out of the old chicken house to further subsidise our incomes. We certainly did not expect to be able to take in paying guests for another two years. After all, the earliest we could find a reliable roofer to replace our leaking roof was not until mid-winter,

The chicken house

and there was not a single pane of glass in any of the second floor windows.

The arrival of Tess and her friend Jane on our doorstep, hoping to camp out in our building site came as an awful shock. Faye could only offer them a vacant ground floor room which had a spring beneath its floor, and was liable to flood if it rained hard. Both girls were only too glad to find it had a double bed, which Faye hurriedly made up for them. That evening the girls wisely decided to walk down to town for a meal at the Hotel Moderne. They returned very late, well fed and rather the worse for drinking too many glasses of the local red wine. They were very tired after their walk back in the dark and fell into bed without paying any attention to their makeshift bedroom.

Next morning many hours after the cock had crowed, they woke bleary eyed and surveyed their sun-soaked surroundings which no doubt resembled a run down prison cell. To their horror two gendarmes were leering at them through the iron barred windows. Tessa said,

'My God, we must have been so drunk we were arrested, and spent the night in a prison cell.'

An hour or so later Alan, Faye and I were entertaining some friends in the salon on the first floor, when the double doors were thrown back and in strode the two armed gendarmes, who promptly demanded our passports, and then questioned us as to who we were exactly. 'How many are there of you who reside here?' the senior one demanded. I told him there were only three of us, just as the two girls stepped into the salon to join the throng.

The senior gendarme looked confused, but he did remember to return our passports before he and his sidekick left.

Some years later I was told, in the strictest confidence, that Gendarmes keep records of all those living in their commune. I would have been very interested to know what they made of the folk who lived in Le Mas Pradel.

Tess and Jane enjoyed their 'camping inside holiday'. Tess's sister Liz and her partner stayed with us as paying guests a year or so later, when much of the renovations had been completed, and they too enjoyed a very lively time with us.

Our first party

After months of very hard work on the house, Faye decided it was about time for us to let our hair down, and she suggested that it would be a good idea to invite all the folk who had helped us in so many ways since we had arrived in Saint Ambroix. It would also show our new-found friends just how much we appreciated being welcomed into their commune.

By this time our kitchen, salon and cloakroom were just about presentable, but the room we planned to be our future dining room was the one which Tess and Jane thought was a prison cell, and it was going to be for 'Strictly Come Dancing'.

Faye and Alan set to work installing dimmed and coloured lighting, and removing the chairs, so that everybody would be on their feet, and providing suitable lively music to get the guests moving. The kitchen was reserved for eating and drinking, and the salon was to be reserved as a retreat from the noise, where conversation could be heard and enjoyed.

By the time our hostess had welcomed all of our numerous guests the party was well under way, and I was very surprised that our guests from all walks of way mixed very well. There were no inhibitions on the dance floor or anywhere else for that matter. A young couple who lived on the *route nationale*, at the beginning of our private road, gave a superb demonstration of rock and roll, which set the pace for the rest of the dancers.

Fortunately it had not rained for some time, which saved us the embarrassment of distributing twenty-eight containers to catch the rainwater which poured through the roof, and providing wellies for those wishing to try dancing on a waterlogged floor.

Faye, Alan and I enjoyed seeing everyone in a party spirit, be it Scotch or wine, but we were very glad to retreat to the salon for some restful conversations with those who had bagged the comfortable armchairs. The evening was a success, and it was the forerunner of many others at Le Mas Pradel.

I recall the estate agent who sold our house and his wife discussing how the three of us would fit into the local social sets, they had a good laugh as they considered us joining various societies, and decided that none of them would suit us. They finally told us that whatever happened to us, Le Mas Pradel would certainly be a house of notoriety. It had already reached that distinction.

5

The Work Begins

The leaking roof

Mr Roux our builder had earmarked the renewal of our roof for the mid-winter. He assured us that it would be perfectly normal to undertake roof renewals at this time, because there would not be any rain or snow then. Unfortunately he had been unable to find a carpenter to do the structural support work, so I agreed to do the work myself. We had had enough of collecting the rain which leaked through our sieve-like roof, and we worried about the rainy season.

The arrival of the tower crane heralded the start of one major project which was long overdue. However, the work hit the buffers because we had no legal access to the land behind the house where the crane had to be sited.

Our helpful neighbour Daniel, seeing the men were at a standstill, asked Mr Roux what the problem was. He apologised for having to rush off to work, but he told him to get his men to dig up part of his embankment to form a makeshift run-in for the crane. Problem solved!

Having spent several years dealing with truculent owners of properties adjoining my own in a Cornish creekside, who battled tooth and nail for land which belonged to me, I realised the attitudes of my Cornish and French neighbours were as different as chalk and cheese.

I had already determined that the major part of the roof needed extra strengthening, so I had constructed a very robust A frame to reduce the unsupported span by half. Alas, Mr Roux hurried up the steep flights of stairs and arrived out of breath bearing some very unwelcome news. The ancient massive oak frame had rotted over the

One of the A frames which I made can be seen

centuries and needed urgent repairs. My A frame had to be installed elsewhere to save the roof from collapsing, because the purlins were resting on a one and a half inch thick wall, which showed sign of instability.

A large degree of panic stirred Mr Roux and me into frenzied activity. We collected the timber for me to make an additional A frame, which had to be made and installed as quickly as possible. The men removed part of the roof and lowered the timber into the room below, where I sweated gallons making the new frame, which the men installed, thus saving the complete roof from collapsing.

The following day three men assisted me in lifting and positioning the heavy timbers into position. I was perched some forty feet or more above ground, balanced precariously working with a small chainsaw, and trying to communicate my instructions to my helpers who only spoke an ancient language used by the Cevenole mountain folk.

Two days later, when two-thirds of the roof had been renewed, Mr Roux decided to remove the last section of the roof. Faye had been hard at work cleaning and polishing everything in the salon and the dining room. The three of us scrubbed up well and made ourselves ready for a swing round a lamp post in Alès which is our nearest town. Just as our feet stepped out of our front door, a tremendous thunder of falling masonry, followed by a thick black cloud of dust, came down the staircase. It was so black and thick it was impossible to see across the stair well. Every thing became covered in the dust and debris, including ourselves as we set-to clearing our path up the stairs to find out what had happened.

The family bedroom, below the section of the roof which was taken down, caused the ceiling to collapse taking with it some tonnage of brick tiles and plaster. The accumulation of so many centuries of soot, dirt, birds' nests and unimaginable junk was not a pretty sight, nor were we when we had cleaned the house up. Three chimney sweeps would have been a good description of us. But it was the workmen who had to carry the rubbish downstairs.

That evening the bedroom was left open to the skies, and it was very cold. Just past midnight it began to snow very heavily. Alan insisted that I telephoned our builder, or rather our demolition expert, to tell him the good news that the bedroom was gradually filling with snow. The poor man arrived with two bleary-eyed workers, and tarpaulins. We woke next morning to find that the tarpaulins had saved well over a foot of snow from soaking the room.

Mr Roux eventually presented his account for our splendid new roof. Alan spotted an error in the account which showed that he had undercharged by a substantial amount. We of course paid the full amount, which stood us in a good light. Word soon got around that we were honest British folk.

The three of us decided to dress up warmly and set off to visit our delightful town, and it was a real joy to walk in the virgin snow all the way down the *route nationale*. The tracks of a skier, and a snow man who was keeping guard outside the pharmacy, were the only signs of life in town.

A treasure hunt

During the rebuilding of a short flight of steps which led to our smallest bedroom on the third floor, which was previously used for keeping pigeons, I discovered a small cache which contained a fossilised human knee bone. I showed it to Alan and Faye but neither of them

Alan at work in the coach house

nor I could make out what it was doing under the steps. It remained in the kitchen for a while and was a topic of conversation with our numerous visitors. However, it went missing one day and we could not think of any reason for its disappearance.

One of our French visitors was horrified to learn that the bone had left the house, because it was the custom to give a treasured relic of a saint to religious houses, and to lose it would bring misfortune on the household. Our visitor pointed to a small cross which had been carved on our front door, which seemed to confirm the connection with the church.

The master bedroom

Several months later Alan's sister Judy discovered our 'saint's bone' whilst digging in the garden. We assumed it was Kate our spaniel who must have found it too hard to eat, so she buried it. All our friends were very relieved to learn that I had hidden it in the house once again, ensuring our good luck would continue.

Daniel eventually related a story about the death of a grandfather who had sold a large part of his estate, and had received payment in gold coins. As he lay dying on his bed surrounded by his family, one of the men asked him where he had hidden his gold. The poor soul was unable to speak or move his hands, but he was able to raise his head and stare at the ceiling before he died. Naturally the room above was searched, and then the entire house, but no matter how thoroughly everybody searched over the house, the treasure was never found.

Our Dutch friend Gus lent us his metal detector, which we used throughout the house, starting in the family bedroom which was the room indicated by the old man. Within a few minutes of scanning the room, the detector emitted a loud signal. Eureka! we had hit the jackpot! The floor tiles were lifted and the only thing we found was aluminium foil stuck to the underside of the tile in question.

Our neighbours remained curious about our searches in the Mas, in case we had found the family, 'treasure'. Several years later I noticed that some floor tiles in the salon were loose and needed fixing. I was surprise to find that one of them had a piece of string attached to its underside. And lo and behold a perfectly formed rectangular hole was beneath the tile with its string. Alan, Faye and I were very excited to have discovered something very unusual. Alan fixed a mirror onto the end of a bamboo cane and lowered his contraption into the hole. Torchlight illuminated a priest hole which was lined with straw. A strong draught of fresh air ventilated the hideout through gaps in the stonework of the outer wall. The actual space used for the priest hole was where the vaulted ceiling met the outer wall, and it provided ample space for someone to sleep in relative comfort.

The access was equally cleverly concealed behind a large picture hung on the staircase wall next to the half landing. It would have been quickly blocked up with a few brick tiles and then plastered over, and the picture rehung, before the soldiers came to root out the protestants and take the priest away to be executed in the most barbaric manner. A lucky priest could easily survive for long periods on the food and water which was lowered to the anxious resident.

Faye's artistic touch! Entrance to Priest Hole

THE WORK BEGINS

Faye is sitting where the Priest's Hole is beneath her chair

It was very strange for me to have discovered two priest holes in my life, and the odds on anyone finding two hitherto undiscovered ones must be greater than winning the lottery. The other one was equally well concealed. However the story of my riverside cottage and its history, which most probably started off as a Cornish long house, would take ages to relate. I hope one day to write the history of the Steward's House of the Manor Sanctuary.

Panning for gold, was an activity organised by an expert in mineralogy, who was a member of The English Speaking Circle. The weather was ideal, the small river was shaded from the summer sunshine, and the small crowd of enthusiastic members were raring to find some gold. The outing was a great success, and even the youngsters enjoyed playing about in the water. Some of us were lucky enough to find some gold, but none of it was any larger than a grain of sugar. However, we had found a way of life in France far more valuable than gold.

Our kitchen

The one room in the house to which everybody gravitated was of course our kitchen, but in the early days it was in desperate need of a new floor and a structural tie to strengthen the outer walls, and provide support for the sagging ceiling and floor above.

My solution was to build three brick pillars, and then build two arches. On top I would cast a reinforced concrete beam which would be keyed into the front and back stone walls of the house. I had built the three pillars and the first arch which had been made on a former given to me by Daniel. I left my work feeling pleased with the progress I had made and joined the others for our evening meal.

Halfway through Faye's delicious pot roast there was an almighty sound of falling masonry which made me think that part of the house had fallen down. A glance in the kitchen confirmed that the house was still standing, but all that was left of my lovely arch was a pile of bricks and mortar on our new floor. However, I managed to complete the structure using extra props, and once the new arch had set the remainder of the work was completed without any mishaps.

The beam propped up the floor above, and it acted as a foundation for the first floor bathroom wall, which in turn supported the floor above. I must own up to feeling rather smug when all the work, including the fitting out, was complete. That's one less room which will not need any more work done on it, or so I thought.

A year later it rained so hard the hillside behind the Mas was flooded with deep water which cascaded into the deep gully behind the house. The water forced its way through the stonework, flooding the kitchen floor. Faye and her friend tried their hardest to empty the kitchen of the rainwater, while Alan and I struggled to clear the drains and gullies. The rain continued to come down like oversized stair rods, so we were unable to redirect the small river which was getting bigger all the time, Alan was so anxious to empty his buckets of water he did not realise that he was filling my wellies. The noise of the cascade and the falling rain was so loud that it drowned my protests. I retreated indoors for a long overdue cup of coffee.

Whilst I sipped the life giving nectar I faced the fact that the only way to prevent rain entering through the gaps in the stonework was to renew the entire pointing of the north-facing wall. This would mean that I would have to do the work myself as our budget would not extend to paying a builder, or for scaffolding.

It was hard work standing on our tallest ladder trying to hold a bucket of mortar, a mortar board, and wield trowels at the same time. Working at the highest level was positively dangerous. Nevertheless it was very satisfying work and as I was working in the shade I was avoiding temperatures which can exceed forty degrees centigrade.

Some like it hot?

Our first season for paying guests was a steep learning curve in the kitchen, because Faye's menu included many full roasted meals. Her cooking arrangements obviously did not rely on the Aga, but the gas cooker and the electric spit roaster-cum-oven were in constant use. Faye, our patron, chef, but not the bottle washer, thrived in the summer heat, but even she began to wilt cooking in temperatures above 100 degrees centigrade. Alan kept two fans directed towards the chef with ice packs to cool the flow of air, so that she wouldn't melt.

Faye, our patron

Faye and I prepared the breakfast table before leaving every morning before nine o'clock because the heat became unbearable an hour later and she needed to keep the food nice and fresh. It did not take long before we began to copy the French summer routine, which means starting work as early as possible, then stopping sharp on midday. A light lunch follows with a modest glass of red wine before taking a siesta until four pm, when everything starts up again. Shops and other businesses remain open for at least a couple of hours. Socialising at all levels from the teenagers to the grown-ups continues until the evening, when mothers expect the whole family to be ready for the main meal of the day and everybody is expected to join in the conversations.

There are other times when the town is devoid of any signs of human life and that is when it rains hard, there is snow falling, or the midday bell is sounded. But once we had become acclimatised to avoiding the summer sunshine, we found the weather was even better than we had hoped for when we planned our move to Saint Ambroix.

However many of our guests wanted to work on their sun tans regardless of the danger of sunstroke. One in particular was in such a bad shape that Faye had to use her medical skills to avoid the dangerous consequences, which can be fatal. She spent the night sponging the poor man down to lower his temperature. There were going to be many of our friends and others who would pop into our kitchen for a consultation about some medical problem. It became a standing joke that the market day was Faye's surgery day.

Faye's surgery

There were other occasions when her so-called patients would pop in for 'a wee bit of advice', and she would usher them into the kitchen for a cup of tea and then listen to their problems. Our paying guests also had problems which sometimes necessitated visiting our family doctor, who didn't speak any English whatsoever. Faye would brief me about the patient's problem. I would then accompany them into the doctor's surgery, where I did my best to translate what Faye had told me about the patient, and what the patient was trying to explain to the doctor. This sometimes made both the doctor and I see the funny side. Nevertheless our Doctor Gorgas was very competent and always solved the problems.

One Christmas time one of our non-paying guests treated everybody staying with us to oysters. Faye had persuaded me to take Jacqueline, who was a delightful French wife of a well-known American architect, to Marseille airport, because she was going to New York for an operation on her eyes.

We had arranged our rendezvous at her home in Alès for 1 am. However, a very thick fog began to slow me down, and I began to feel I had the makings of an upset stomach. Perhaps it was the oysters? Fortunately my son Paul was keeping me company so I asked him to drive on the way back because I was feeling ill. The journey turned out to be a nightmare, because Jacqueline had told me the time of departure was the take-off time of the flight which left Paris, and not Marseille. We were unlikely to be in time unless I drove as fast as possible in the fog.

We arrived at the gate to find all the passengers were already on board, but as there was nobody to stop her she ran like an Olympic athlete, and managed to reach the aircraft just as the door was about to close.

My long walk to the nearest WC was one of the most painful experiences imaginable, as I only just made it in time to relieve me of my first bout of the runs. I was in no condition to drive, so I was thankful Paul drove me home.

The bad news on our return home was that only one of our guests had avoided eating the oysters, and fortunately it was Paul who escaped joining the queue for an injection. Faye told me that Doctor Gorgas had responded very quickly to her urgent telephone call. He only charged the three of us for his call out and injections, which must have put him out of pocket.

I remember his first visit to our house when he was called out to one of our visitors who had been poorly for several days. Having prescribed her medication, he popped his head round the kitchen door and said, 'She didn't speak French, I didn't understand her English, and I hope she survives.'

Despite our difficulties with communication in the early days, the three of us remained very good friends with him throughout our time in France. From that time onwards, Faye made a habit of sending me to accompany her 'patients' who didn't speak French to the doctor for his expert help, as my French was usually required.

100 francs or 10,000 francs

I was surprised to see a brand new Mercedes drive into our courtyard, and I could not put a name to its owner. A tall well-dressed woman stepped out of her car, strode purposely towards our front door and immediately launched herself into her tale of woe. Faye being a sympathetic listener took the brunt of her verbal assault.

She said that her husband and herself were broke and couldn't even find enough cash to pay for their food, and their poor dog hadn't any food either. Faye gave her something to eat for their evening meal, and I gave her £20 pounds-worth of francs for the dog's food, on the understanding that it was to be repaid. Having found that we were a soft touch, she then demanded 10,000 francs as a loan to keep her financially afloat. Faye began to lose her cool, and said she hadn't that kind of money to spare, and even if she had, on no account would she lend it to her. Having her demands refused, the woman lost her temper completely, she jumped into her expensive car and drove off at high speed.

During my regular visit to the family doctor I recounted the above events, which Faye and I found very disturbing as her behaviour was so abnormal. The doctor told me that both the husband and his wife drove new Mercedes cars and had recently spent a huge amount installing a large swimming pool. Obviously the doctor knew the couple's circumstances, and the wife's medical history which was strictly confidential. His parting words to me were, 'Believe me it will all end like a Greek tragedy'.

The ungrateful woman never repaid the loan, and we never saw her again. Did it all end for her as the doctor predicted? I wonder!

George

One market day Faye and I set off on our regular stroll down to town to enjoy the bustle of the market. We left Alan seated in his favourite dining room armchair, with Jasper the border terrier perched on one arm, and Katie our spaniel perched on the other arm. *The Times* was within easy reach, and Alan was a picture of contentment. Faye and I always enjoyed the routine of gathering the freshest vegetables and the ripe fruits, before treating ourselves to spring rolls, from a charming oriental young woman. This time she had a very lively rabbit for sale.

Faye was very upset to be told that the fine specimen would be ideal for a tasty *lapin au moutard*. I was persuaded that we should buy the rabbit and give it to Alan who was bound to be delighted with our gift. He would make an interesting pet.

George and Jasper

Our reception on our return home was not at all enthusiastic when Alan was presented with his new pet, because of all the extra work involved in keeping it well fed and exercised. Nevertheless George the rabbit soon became part of our extended family, and enjoyed his generous sized run, and his hutch with its own stairs to his bedroom. A diet of large clover flowers, succulent lettuce, milk and cornflakes soon put weight on him. Alan even took George for walkies with his own collar and lead, much to the annoyance of the dogs, but they soon made a habit of visiting the new member of the family. It wasn't long before the local rabbits started calling on him during the night. No doubt they all wondered at his size which soon grew from size large to XXL.

Very early one sunny morning I opened the front door to let the dogs out. They came thundering down the stone staircase and into the courtyard at breakneck speed towards a crowd of rabbits who were warming themselves in the rising sun. The dogs approached their breakfast at speed, but then began to slow down so much they resembled a pair of OAPs taking a casual stroll. The rabbits finally scattered and even then our intrepid hunters couldn't be bothered to give chase.

Not long afterwards, Daniel our neighbour, and Chief of Municipal Police, was approaching our friendly crowd of rabbits in his car, together with his colleague. He said, 'You will never believe it but the British rabbits will not even bother to get out of our way.' I witnessed the two policemen doubled up laughing at having to stop and wait for the rabbits to stop sunbathing before they could go on duty.

The cottage

THE WORK BEGINS

One morning Faye was passing the open door to our cottage carrying a tray with milk, cornflakes and water. The father of the family who had rented the cottage asked Faye where she was going. 'I am taking George his breakfast,' she replied. Our tenant replied, 'I didn't know you took guests down there,' as he pointed towards our lean-to garage where George resided. Little did he realise that it was a rabbit who enjoyed his four star accommodation, and his breakfast in bed.

Twice a year the three of us returned to the UK to visit our respective families and friends, which necessitated finding a friend to look after our home, and to take care of George, who was dieting so well he could enter the Guinness Book of Records as the largest of his kind. Fortunately our friend John was always delighted to have the company of our dogs, and he walked them so far in the open countryside every day that their legs seemed a little shorter when he reluctantly returned them. He was so fond of his four-legged friends that he insisted on keeping them for an extra day.

Pearl, a Kentish girl and member of the English Circle, was given the use of our house and cottage during our absences, in return for a promise to look after George in the style to which he had been accustomed. Faye always remembered to give Pearl a worthwhile present if she found the house still standing.

One of our homecomings was a sad affair. During our absence one of our friends popped in to see us, and was disappointed to find we were not due home for a week or so. She was horrified to see Pearl in a very distressed state, and saying repeatedly, 'I have killed George. What will they say when they come home?'

Poor Pearl had forgotten to room service George's apartment, and our pet had died of starvation and lack of liquid in his mini bar. The three of us, the dogs, the rabbits from the local warren and many of our visitors, missed George's company for many months and we still remember our friend to this day.

6

Some Risky Outings

Dangers on the road to Uzes

Most of the time in the early days was devoted to restoring the Mas which was very hard physical work, so we took time out and treated ourselves to touring the local unspoilt and fascinating countryside.

This particular day we chose to visit Uzes some 30 miles or so to the south of Saint Ambroix because it was the market day, and it was very popular with the tourists. We enjoyed soaking up the ambience and numerous cups of coffee, before purchasing several books from an Englishman who had settled in the town.

Several days before our outing Daniel our neighbour warned me, 'All the crooks in the north of France take their holidays in the south, where they combine their business with pleasure.' He also said that bandits contrived to stop foreign cars, and use violence to strip the owners of anything they can find of value. His advice was not to stop even for an apparent accident in lonely situations.

On leaving the town the road home runs downhill for several miles between rows of large shade trees which are very picturesque. We had barely left the town when a car pulled up alongside us, and the unpleasant-looking men in it seemed to be staring at us. They seemed to be making their minds up to try and stop us. Sure enough the driver then tried to push us off the road between the trees.

I remembered Daniel's advice about not stopping in lonely situations, even if there appears to be an accident, or something looks out of place. I jammed my foot on the accelerator and kept it there until we had managed to get well ahead of the hijackers. Rallying had been my sport and I had taken part in three national events, so I was only doing what I enjoyed doing, driving fast on difficult roads, which certainly saved us from being the next victims of those crooks.

The hitch-hiker

Several years after our brush with the bandits, Faye and I set off once again on the road to Uzes, but this time it was to meet my son Paul at Avignon, some forty kilometres further on. Paul's visits always brought a breath of fresh air, with his sense of humour, so I was enjoying the drive to Uzes even more than usual, with the prospect of seeing Paul again.

Halfway along the road to Uzes I spotted a hitch-hiker who looked dejected and was clasping a plastic bag. I was in a good mood and I felt sorry for the figure who was sweltering in the sunshine. I pulled over and asked the young man, who was about the same age and build as my son, where he was going. Much to my surprise he hadn't made up his mind. I told him where we were heading, and he said, 'That's all right I suppose.' He opened the rear door and sat down without saying anything else.

I watched our passenger in my rear view mirror, because I felt that something was not normal in his behaviour. He was sweating profusely and kept holding his plastic bag as though his life depended upon its contents.

It didn't take long for me to realise that I had made one very serious mistake in letting a deranged hitch-hiker get into my car. I decided that his plastic bag contained some sort of weapon, and my problem was how to get rid of this nutter, without letting him injure Faye and me. The safest solution was to drive into the centre of Uzes, which would be very crowded because it was market day, and there would be safety in numbers.

I stopped in the middle of town without giving any indication of my plans. I opened the rear door and told him to get out, whilst keeping my eyes glued to his hands, which I was certain held a revolver. We drove off in haste towards Avignon, and for the first time since I had given the hitch-hiker a lift, we were able to discuss the incident without any fear. Faye's nursing experience of dealing with psychiatric patients confirmed that we had been in real danger on the road to Uzes.

Paul arrived on time on the TGV, and we enjoyed our reunion in the station buffet before retracing our road back home, without expecting any more problems.

As we approached the spot where we picked up our hitch-hiker, an armed gendarme signalled me to stop. During my interrogation which followed, I sensed that he was expecting trouble by the way he fingered his holster and the butt of his revolver. His first question was whether I had given a hitch-hiker a lift at the very spot where we had stopped. Next he wanted me to explain who Paul was, and what he was doing in my car.

Once I had satisfied my inquisitor of our bona fides, the gendarme explained that a man of similar age and build had murdered someone and a manhunt was in progress. The plastic bag no doubt contained the murder weapon, and we were lucky to escape being two more victims.

Coloured lightning

Our regular family visitors who travelled on the TGV, would avail themselves of our free taxi service from Avignon to Saint Ambroix via Uzes. Faye's son David offered to accompany Faye and me in his own car with his wife and son by way of an outing.

This journey proved to be anything other than an enjoyable trip through the countryside, because as we approached our destination the sky was being lit up by what looked like a severe electrical storm unlike any other I had seen. Even crossing the Bay of Biscay in a tropical cyclonic storm, with continuous fork lightning, shooting stars, and stormforce seas, didn't worry me as much as our drive home when the storm was at its zenith.

Coloured lightning continued to run across the open and lonely countryside with pink, greens, and blues, which illuminated the land in such a way that it would have been an ideal scene for a weird and creepy late night film. The smell of burning electricity permeated the car. I began to expect the car to be struck, and I started to look for a safe refuge. Alas! There were no friendly lights to be seen anywhere on the barren road to Uzes.

I decided to press on as quickly as possible, trusting that we would not be the victims of God's *son et lumière*. I kept my eyes glued to the rear mirror to make sure David was keeping pace with us, as it was reassuring to be in his company, although it wouldn't reduce our risk of being hit.

We were on the same downhill road where the hijackers tried to force us off the road, when the low misty sky turned bright pink. A pink ball of lightning hit the tarmac no more than a foot or so in front of our bumper! David and I continued driving through the nightmare conditions as fast as possible until we reached the safety of our very substantial stone house.

Some weeks later we returned our visitors to Avignon railway station, so I had the opportunity to check if the ball of fire had damaged the tarmac. I was relieved to see a three-metre circular burn in the tarmac, because it confirmed that I hadn't dreamed the nightmare journey on the road to Uzes. David told me that he was sure that we had been hit because the whole of our car was enveloped by the falling pink ball of lightning.

It crossed my mind each time I used the same road that we had survived several dangerous incidents, and I wondered if there would be any more in store for us.

Lost at night in the forest

Alan's health had been declining for some time, although for the last eight years he had been very active. He had installed the electricity and the plumbing in the house and our cottage. He also designed a drainage system which kept the entire ground floor free from rising water. Faye also helped with some of the donkeywork of laying the concrete floor.

Faye had noticed that Alan had slowed down, and was less enthusiastic about travelling, so it came as a surprise when he suddenly informed us that we must visit Chateau Montelet. He wasn't going to be put off when I told him the footpath, which led directly over the steep hill behind the Mas, had been left overgrown for some years, and it was impossible to use this short cut.

He said that it must be possible to approach the chateau from the river valley, although any path would be very steep indeed. Nothing was going to dissuade him, and he said, 'It is the last thing I want to do.'

The autumn was closing in and with the longer nights, this particular day it was leaving us barely enough time to attempt the climb up the steep valley side to the grassy plateau where the chateau was sited. We couldn't find the proper path and Alan started to scramble up the wooded slope. I could see that he was all fired up at the prospect of reaching his destination. Faye and I were both alarmed because he was more than likely going to fall. Nevertheless he led the way and we finally reached the plateau more by good luck than by good judgement.

The ruin of the chateau was a gem, and had the air of being a fairytale castle. Even Jasper and Katie were excited at the prospect of another interesting adventure. Before we set off to investigate our new find, Faye and I stressed that we would meet up at the beginning of the proper path which led down the steep hill to where our car was parked, and we would only be able to spend a very short time inside the ruins.

Our visit proved to be well worth the effort of climbing the valley, and collecting some scratches on the way, but there remained very little time before the twilight reminded us that we would have to descend the steep path in the dark if we didn't hurry up. I returned to the meeting point and found Faye and the dogs waiting impatiently for Alan and me. I returned to the ruins and called out that we must leave, but Alan was so enthralled with his visit he refused to go. I tried again but this time there was no response so we told the dogs to go and find their father. They returned quickly, without him.

He was nowhere in sight or within shouting distance, so we were well and truly in the mire as we would be unable to find him in the dark. My choice was to take Faye and the dogs back to the car, and if Alan wasn't there I would drive home and leave them waiting beside the telephone. I then visited the HQ of the Emergencies Service in Saint Ambroix to get help.

Faye telephoned a very close friend called Heather and told her what had happened to Alan. Her response was not what she expected. 'At least Alan got his last wish.' Heather did arrive within ten minutes and she provided Faye with some moral support, which she sadly needed.

It took at least ten minutes for me to explain what had happened to Alan in sufficient detail for the Controller to relay the importance of finding an elderly man who was no doubt wandering about somewhere in the forest, without even a pocket torch, or enough warm clothing. I listened intently to the Controller as he instructed four teams of two-manned four-wheel-drive vehicles, to start the search starting where Alan was last seen at the chateau. The railway which passes close to the spot where our car had been parked was closed and a special vehicle was called on to assist in searching part of the Ceze valley. In addition the Alès dog handler was put on standby. I was very impressed by the way the Controller had got the search under way.

However, I was surprised when the senior gendarme from the local HQ started to question me in such detail that he appeared to suspect I might have reason to murder Alan. Fortunately the three of us were well known, and we had a good reputation in the town, and I wasn't in the habit of losing my best friends.

While I was still waiting in the HQ of the emergency services, a message came through the loudspeaker saying that a gentleman had been seen walking towards a small cafe, with the aid of a walking stick, and wearing a straw hat. I was asked if that description might fit Alan Greene. The Deputy Mayor politely asked me if Alan was related to Graham Greene, because he thought there was a strong resemblance. I told him that he was a second cousin, hence the likeness.

I was elated to hear the good news that Alan was on his way home uninjured, and was being escorted by the mayor in the ambulance which had collected Alan from the the cafe. Alan was suffering from exhaustion from walking many miles before finding a young lad outside his home, who directed him towards civilisation not far from where we had parked the car. Poor Alan had to suffer the indignity of having to ask the owner of the cafe for a coffee but was unable to pay for it.

Faye and I were relieved when Alan was safely tucked up in bed with his dogs curled up beside him, and we contemplated how grateful we were for all the support we had been given.

7

Local Characters

John Palmer

One evening at The English Speaking Circle, John asked if he could join our Association, which met every Thursday evening, except during the summer months. On the face of it he was a promising member, well educated and with a very responsible managerial post in the EDF. Unfortunately he was sweating with embarrassment and he was very nervous. Faye took him under her wing and tried to put him at ease, which was no mean task. After he had attended several meetings he took a liking to the three of us, and invited us to visit his home in Alès.

Members of The English Circle called us the folk from the English manor house

His conducted tour of the industrial building which had been converted into his home was an eye opener because it contained every facility one could dream of. A private cinema, a games room with billiard tables, table tennis, a workshop with every piece of equipment and machinery imaginable, a drive-in garage for ten cars, and all of this was fitted comfortably in the ground floor.

The first floor reception-cum-lounge looked like the interior of a Disneyworld castle, with a full-sized professional organ, and gallery. Its decor was in keeping although I didn't notice any knights in armour hiding in the alcoves. The rest of the accommodation was arranged around the ornamental garden with its water feature, and private entrance to the local park.

There was no doubt that our new member was a brilliant model maker, because he had made the most perfect working model of a helicopter, which was so valuable he planned to learn to fly a real one before he dared to fly his model. The only fly in the ointment was his collection of working puppets that he kept on display in one of the basement corridors, which I found to be very eerie.

John invited us to take tea and sample his own homemade cake. However, we found it strange that his wife did not join us, which indicated that all was not well with John's marriage.

For a while John missed The English Speaking Circle meetings. It came as a pleasant surprise when he suddenly turned up at the Mas to invite us to go flying with him, in his new light aircraft from a small airfield near La Grande Combe. He had decided to take up flying his own aircraft instead of learning to fly helicopters, and kept his wonderful model in mothballs instead. His visit to the Mas was the last time we saw John, and it was months later when meetings restarted after the summer break that we were told of our friend's demise. He had taken off from his usual airfield in fog and deliberately crashed his aircraft.

It was our opinion that he couldn't bear to be without his wife, who had died, and his daughter who had thrown herself out of her window and hadn't survived.

Dowsing and divining

One of The English Circle guests gave a most interesting talk and demonstration of the art of divining and dowsing. Although I accepted that water sources can be found by dowsers, using a simple Y-shaped hazel branch, her divining with the aid of a gold ring suspended by a fine thread, which acted as a pendulum, appeared to have some strange powers. Although the guest seemed to overestimate the powers, I decided to try my own hand at dowsing using two L-shaped wire rods, and follow her instructions to see if there was any explanation for the way the system works.

The L-shaped pieces of coathanger wire must be held gently, and they should point ahead as the searcher walks towards his intended objective. Imagine my surprise when I made my first attempt to find the source of the Mas Pradel well. The rods turned towards the right and then crossed themselves as I reached the source of the well. It was this event which kickstarted my interest in dowsing.

I happened to mention to my son-in-law that I could detect water using my L-shaped rods, but he only laughed and said that he didn't believe me. Alan suggested that he could devise a test that would settle the argument. He arranged a tray full of tumblers and only one of them was full of water, and then he covered the tumblers with a sheet of cardboard. I was then sent out of the room while Jack my son-in-law positioned the water-filled tumbler. As there wasn't any suitable wire to make the rods, I chose to use my daughter's wedding ring and a length of cotton to make a pendulum which I was to hold, and then pass it over the cardboard cover. No one was more surprised than me when it started to gyrate, and it was exactly over the water-filled tumbler.

Encouraged by my success I attempted to find a pipe which was under the floorboards. I did get a very strong reaction which led me to trace the position of the pipe, which turned out to be an iron gas pipe. I noticed that as I approached the hidden pipe the pendulum was stationary, but moved towards the pipe and hung defying the laws of gravity, as the cotton was leaning towards the pipe. This strange phenomenon was attested by my three onlookers.

Another demonstration Faye and I had witnessed was the power of recognising the difference between healthy food and substances which are decidedly unhealthy. Alan arranged some dessert bowls which were filled with a selection of these foods, cigarettes, alcohol, and sundry other samples. These bowls were then covered with the cardboard. Each time the pendulum began to rotate, Alan marked the spot with the direction the pendulum rotated. Each sample of healthy foods rotated the pendulum clockwise, and the unhealthy items caused the pendulum to rotate anticlockwise. These demonstrations finally put Jack's scepticism to bed.

Our friend Mai Zetterling was so impressed with what she had learned about divining from the English Circle guest, she invited her to visit Le Mazel, because she hoped divining could solve a mystery. It concerned a young girl who supposedly was bricked up in the basement of her home, which certainly had the spooky atmosphere.

Alan and I carefully surveyed all the nooks and crannies in the basement, and we were unable to find any walls which were thick enough to accommodate even a small hell hole. There were no signs of abnormality in the brickwork, nor did we meet the ghost of the young girl.

My own conclusion as to the bona fides of the diviner was called into question, when we found that she was making up all sorts of stories, which had little or no connection to her skill as a diviner. One such claim was that she could ask the pendulum a question and it would respond in yes or no mode depending on the direction of its rotation. The price of her services no doubt depended upon the guile of the diviner. In this instant Mai seemed to believe some of the nonsense about the ghost which the diviner embellished. Alan and I decided that we would not tell Mai what we believed. After all, the story gives the rambling old house a certain cachet.

Creepy crawlies and nasties

Our temporary holiday house, Les Volets Rouge, had introduced us to the black scorpions who had taken up residence when the property was left vacant. The nightly ritual was to check that any scorpions were exterminated before going to bed. The morning ritual was to bang shoes to dislodge any of the little blighters who may have slept in. It was also advisable to shake clothes before wearing them. Take care not to disturb flat stones, as you are likely to be stung. Faye had the misfortune to be stung twice simply because she was wearing sandals.

When we moved into Le Mas Pradel my very first job was to clear out a large understairs store, prior to converting it into a cloakroom with our only WC. The part underneath the stairs was filled with dank, smelly rubbish, which was home to the most revolting sinister creepy crawlies I had ever seen. I decided the easiest and safest way to deal with the problem was simply to brick up the opening and starve the horrid creatures.

We had barely settled into our semi-derelict building, in fact we were sleeping in the house for the first time, when a noise of falling heavy objects woke us all up with a start. The sound came from the old silk room on the third floor. I leaped out of bed and grabbed my First World War bayonet, which I kept handy in case of burglars, and ran up the stairs in my pyjamas to confront the intruder. However, the burglar turned out to be a strange animal the size of an obese stoat. I chased it, brandishing my executioner's style sword, until I had it cornered, but it ran up the opened door of the pigeon loft where it sat on top of the door and stared at me with evil intent. I raised my weapon, but the interloper had sense enough to make a desperate leap through the open window, leaving behind a ridiculous-looking figure whose pyjama bottoms had fallen down.

Several months later the household was woken by a hideous growling, coming from the first floor terrace. I opened the door wide enough to see what I was told were mountain animals, two or three times larger than domestic cats. The broom I had armed myself with was totally inadequate to protect myself, so I wisely closed the door, and left these ferocious creatures to carry on mating. We had enough sense to ignore these creatures when they returned once more the following season.

Gradually we became accustomed to living with God's creatures with the exception of Montpellier snakes which avoided us for some reason. Eventually I came face to face with one of these three-foot snakes which had entwined itself through the trellis at the front door.

This one seemed quite at home and was not at all concerned with me. I reasoned that in any event it would be unable to strike out at me so I stroked it to see what would happen. It remained like a contented dog being petted by its owner.

One extremely hot summer evening, Trevor our seasonal washer-up and friend had barely gone to bed when he came running down the three flights of stairs in a very disturbed state.

'I can't go in there it's full of hornets,' he said pointing up the stairwell.

'You had better go and see what's going on, Richard. You know that you are the dispatcher of all the nasty and dangerous critters, so get cracking,' Faye said, and continued to socialise with the guests.

Meanwhile I opened Trevor's bedroom door very carefully, but enough to see that there were enough hornets to establish a nest. Their behaviour reminded me of the Kamikaze homing in on the US aircraft carriers during the war in the Pacific.

I prudently retired to assess my task of hornet cleansing of Trevor's room. Covering myself completely from top to bottom and wearing gloves and glasses would reduce the risk, and my sturdy swat should do the trick. Fortunately the window was open and the hornets decided they did not like my frantic swatting. One by one I flicked them through the window.

It is widely known that three stings from a hornet can kill a horse, and just one sting on the head will cause the windpipe in a human being to close up, choking the poor victim to death. One of our friend's neighbours died from a single sting from a wasp within a very short time. I consider myself very lucky to survive my brush with so many hornets, who were about to make their nest in Trevor's room.

Le Mas Pradel had been abandoned for such a long time prior to our occupation, the rats and other undesirables had made themselves at home. Alan commented, after he had visited the workshop in the dark using a torch, that he had seen lots of little eyes shining from gaps in the stonework. The following morning I visited George our pet who at that time lived comfortably in his run and hatch in the lean-to garage. However, lots of rats had taken a liking to George and had made their home in the rafters above his run. It was time for me to give them notice to quit. Daniel, our neighbour, collected from the town hall enough rat poison to get rid of our health hazard, and within a few days George's admirers had moved on.

We found a charming blue-coloured animal the size of a rat, but with round-shaped ears, hiding close to George's run. He died shortly after from rat poison.

The surviving rats moved into the loft space above the bathroom in the cottage, which necessitated removing part of the ceiling in order to put the poison in place. The sounds of tiny feet scampering above the ceiling finally stopped disturbing our guests' sleep. We were surprised that none of the guests had commented about the noise.

Large hairy spiders sometimes made the females panic. Jasper, Katie and I usually managed to kill the spiders, who don't do any harm, in fact they feed off flies, mosquitoes and other undesirable insects.

Mice managed to set up home in the bottom of the double sink cabinet, and try as hard as we could, we were unable to get rid of them from the very expensive unit without destroying it. Katie and Jasper earned their keep by hunting, so we let the dogs loose with instructions to get the mice. Suddenly the mice abandoned their cabinet, and the dogs gave chase, but Katie was so anxious to join in the fun, and moved so fast, that she simply slid on the polished floor tiles. Jasper joined in the chaos in a more reasoned way and chased the family of mice out of the front door. Thanks to the dogs' love of hunting the house remained free of mice for the duration of our time in Le Mas Pradel.

John the humorist

This John was a completely different kettle of fish from the previous one. He was a good example of someone who is only rude to his friends, and very rude to his best friends. Our visitors and guests were often appalled at the way he addressed us. For example he referred to Faye as his 'Old Dragon'. If we phoned him to say we would be calling at his bungalow, his reply was 'I'll make sure that I will be out' or 'What makes you think I will be glad to see you?' However, his rudeness was a cover for his real feelings, and he had a mischievous sense of humour.

Ringing our ship's bell at the wrong time was guaranteed to send our paying guests running down to the dining room, only to find the table laid and nothing to eat. Faye usually found enough extra food for him to join our paying guests for the evening meal.

The postman delivered an invitation from the mayor of a small village near John's home, so we suspected it had some connection with our friend. The invitation was typed on official headed notepaper, and requested us to attend a function which was being held near a car park, where we were to join the other invitees. The reason for this function was not at all clear but the three of us decided to attend out of curiosity. When we arrived on time nobody was there. We waited for a good half an hour before we gave up and went to the mayor's office to find out what on earth was going on. The secretary said, 'You should know what the French are like by now, they are always late so I should go back to the car park.'

When we returned to the car park it was obvious that our invitation was to explore the Aven D'Orgnac, because a large sign proclaimed that the huge cavern, and a very deep underground dried up river, was open for visitors. John was standing in a group of guides who had been taught English by our friend. Faye and I were in a group of English visitors who were being used as guinea pigs, so that the guides' command of English could be assessed.

Our guide took us down in a lift to a depth of well over a hundred feet, and then we walked along a tunnel which ended in a huge dome-shaped cavern, the size of the dome of St Paul's Cathedral. Awe-inspiring steps led down to the depths below, where the dried up river bed could be seen, and continued for many miles. On the way towards the steps John suddenly popped out of the gloom and pointed to a very large stalagmite. He said in a loud voice for everyone to hear, 'I thought you would be interested Faye, in seeing another one of your own kind, called The Old Dragon.'

Faye always took John's leg pulling very well, although the guides were not very impressed with his sense of humour.

John always made a point of inviting the three of us to the residential seven-day language courses which were part of the Ecole de Mines curriculum for the students, and our friend was their English tutor for the events. The venues for these courses were held in interesting chateaus which specialised in corporate events. English-speaking visitors gave the students a chance to converse on very interesting and diverse topics. We enjoyed the company of some very bright young men who came from different backgrounds. We also joined in the tutorials and were encouraged to voice our opinions on all sorts of topical subjects.

I remember one of the African students whose intellect impressed me considerably. I asked him what it felt like when he returned to his native village. He was sad at not being able to tell his family about modern technology, because his mother's understanding was so inadequate and caused embarrassment at his inability at not being able to answer many of the questions which the family posed.

Driving home in the middle of a winter's night, on small roads and through the desolate Cevenne mountains, was an experience I wouldn't recommend to the faint hearted.

Towards the end of the academic studies at the Ecole de Mines, a presentation was given by the students who had completed their English Language course, and the presentation was like a passing-out parade to display their prowess. John told Faye that he was concerned that the mother of one of his students was unable to attend this important event, because she lived too far away. He asked Faye if she would take the mother's place to give the poor lad enough confidence to address the audience of parents. His chosen topic was Scotland and The Scots. Faye always came to the rescue of lame ducks, or anybody for that matter who needed help and being Scottish, the topic was enough to pluck at her heart strings, so she agreed to John's request.

Alan was curious about the invitation so all three of us turned up at the assembly hall of the Ecole de Mines. We sat well away from the stage, but close enough for Faye's temporary son to see that his surrogate mother had turned up to watch his presentation. When his turn came he spoke about the strange things the Scots eat and drink, and how they throw themselves about, and hop between crossed swords.

It was at this stage of the presentation that John appeared on stage and announced that Faye Greene had kindly offered to accompany the poor lad who was about to demonstrate one of the most energetic dances, with a real live Scottish lassie. Faye was taken by surprise, but was unable to back out in face of the clapping and shouts of encouragement.

The unlikely couple gave a commendable demonstration of the Highland Fling, to the delight of the audience. Such was John's practical joke, but Faye bade her time before she had her revenge.

Sainte Marie de la Mer

Our favourite visitor had travelled all the way from the Inner Hebrides, to bring some extra joy to our lives at the Mas. Brian is the youngest son of Faye and Alan. He has the gift of making friends wherever he goes, and always has time to help those in trouble, just like his mother, so it was only natural that Faye and I wanted to share a special day with him. Our choice was to visit the Gypsy Festival which was being held at Sainte Marie de la Mer, where gypsies come from all over Europe to celebrate the Festival of the Sea.

The town is situated in the Camargue, which is France's second most important national park. It is renowned for its wild white horses that roam the surrounding flat land, and rice fields flourish. We had chosen a unique spot to live in because our Department had the Cevennes which is France's first national park as well as the Camargue. The drive downhill all the way to the Mediterranean was enjoyable, and I found the only vacant parking place left in town, which was being guarded by two gypsy women. They welcomed us to their festival and gave me a small sea shell as a good luck charm. Was there a catch in our good luck in finding the only parking space, I asked myself?

One of the women came to my open car window and said that as we were attending a religious festival we should make the sign of the cross, using two folded low-denomination notes, which would bless us. She assured me that she had no intention of keeping these notes and would not even touch them. Muggins Bishop only had two 200-franc notes which I folded as she requested. The next second she snatched the only money which I had, and ran away laughing at my stupidity. I now had nothing left to pay for lunch and to top up the petrol tank. We searched in vain for these two crooks without any luck, so I reported my loss to the municipal police who were very sympathetic.

I was asked to identify them from their rogues' gallery, which I did without any hesitation. The senior officer knew the two in question, and asked me to accompany him while he searched the town for them. He also questioned lots of the locals if they had seen these two, who had obvious records for deception. At one stage we entered the church to see if they were hiding amongst the packed out congregation. He told me that these two always changed their top garments after a heist to confuse their identification. He told me that if I was certain that I had correctly identified the gypsy who had snatched my money, the police would set up a road block on the only road in or out of the town, to check the gypsy vehicles for these two women. They would be arrested if they were found.

Having wasted my time looking for the elusive gypsies and my four hundred francs, I decided to return to my car. Suddenly the thief and her accomplice approached me. 'I hear that the police are looking for me,' the one who had snatched my money said. 'I have only two hundred francs of your money because I have already spent the rest,' she added and then thrust the two hundred franc note into my hand before the couple ran away as fast as they could.

I considered what to do about helping the police catch two of the notorious confidence tricksters who had been fleecing the visitors for many years. I returned to the police station where I explained what had happened in the car park, and confirmed my identification of both the wanted women. I was thanked for my cooperation by the senior officer who said that these two tricksters would not be in business again in his town.

My visit to the festival was not at all what I expected, but at least I had enough money to top up the petrol tank, and we got home, having seen the Camargue horses and the rice fields, but with empty stomachs.

8

Gerald and His Camper Van

One glorious summer's day I was feeling very pleased with life at Le Mas Pradel, because the renovations were transforming the old wreck of a building into one fit for accommodating paying guests. Faye had put an advert in *The Lady* magazine which found some very interesting guests. It looked very promising for the future of our private hotel, so we decided that Faye should be the patron of our establishment. It was a wise move because our incomes began to look healthy for the first time since we had bought the property. Our discerning guests made our venture very rewarding and I had come to the conclusion that we had chosen a good lifestyle for our retirement.

Part of the newly rendered façade, 1985

BONNE CHANCE

It came as a let-down to see an ancient VW camper van heading towards our courtyard. I expected to see some hippies looking for cheap bed and breakfast, so I was relieved to see a well-spoken man ask the Lady of the House if he could park somewhere in our grounds. Faye agreed to his request, but made the mistake of not charging for the use of our facilities.

Gerald's excuse for not using one of the many camping sites in the district was that he needed peace and quiet to deal with a tin trunk full of important documents. He parked his camper van close to our kitchen in a small parking lot, and then promptly began work on his papers seated at our garden table. The contents of the trunk were a complete mess and nothing was even filed. He soon lost interest in his jumble of papers, and concentrated on scrounging drinks and whatever food was going spare. However repayment for our generous hospitality came in the form of his life history, which he related to the three of us when we had spare time, or to the paying guests if he was invited to join them for coffee after their meal.

During one evening Gerald joined a medical consultant and his wife for an after meal chat. The conversation turned to Gerald's time spent in Moscow after the war. The consultant did not believe his story, but he soon had to eat his words, because Gerald displayed a remarkable knowledge of the city. The guest was so fascinated with Gerald's stories he investigated his background, and was surprised to find him mentioned in *Who's Who*. His family were titled folk with connections with Ireland.

During 'the troubles' in Ireland Gerald had lived in a bungalow, and I suspect was a British intelligence agent. Unfortunately the IRA realised he was an informer and decided to murder him. The first attempt on his life was a failure because the hit man botched the arranged car accident, but it did make Gerald very careful each time he walked into town. The second attempt was another failure, because one of the Garda told Gerald that the IRA were going to burn his bungalow down whilst he was inside. This gave him a chance to prepare his defence, which was to connect his garden hose to the kitchen tap and feed it though the roof tiles. He didn't have long to wait for the arsonists to arrive carrying their firewood, paper, paraffin and of course matches. Each time they started a fire Gerald sprayed the men and doused the fire, which made the arsonists lose their tempers, but the situation was so absurd Gerald couldn't contain his sense of humour which inflamed the arsonist's frustration beyond belief. They retired, even more determined to kill him. Soon graffiti appeared in town threatening to kill the English informer.

The final attempt on Gerald's life was more serious and it took place in the middle of town in daylight. He was using the only telephone box when a man pushed the door open and stabbed him in the head with a sharpened screwdriver which punctured his skull. Shortly afterwards he was recalled to the UK for further treatment, and he was told not to return to his bungalow in Ireland. This incident was reported in one of the national daily newspapers. Gerald dug deep into his tin trunk and produced a copy of the newspaper for us to read.

Gerald had been in the habit of spending his summers living in his camper van, anywhere in the south of France which took his fancy as long as there was free parking and other free perks. His previous site before he discovered Le Mas Pradel was in the grounds of the Belgian Consul's house. By this time Faye was concerned about Gerald so she telephoned the Consul, and mentioned that she understood that Gerald's sister was married to him. The poor man had been pestered into letting him park his camper van for several summers, and he found it almost impossible to get rid of him. He most certainly was not married to Gerald's sister. We began to realise that Gerald was mentally disturbed and most probably was being treated for this and not for the injury to his head. The first year that he didn't visit Le Mas Pradel, it was autumn before he telephoned us in a very distressed state and needed some medical attention.

At the end of his annual tour of the south of France he had decided to camp out in a nudist camp, which had been shut for the winter. He had planned to cook sausages and mash for his evening meal, but went in search of wild herbs to spice up his dinner. He wandered along the steep and wooded banks of the river, which became a gorge with a very picturesque river glinting in the evening sunset. He was enjoying the warmth of the last of the sunset dressed only in shorts, t-shirt and plimsoles.

He was about to turn back when suddenly the sun dropped below the horizon and within a few minutes he was left in total darkness, stumbling about through the wood and feeling the chill of the night air closing about him. Not being able to see where he was going he found it impossible to avoid being cut and scratched by the thorns and brambles.

Moving a few feet at a time he tried to feel his way back to the path which followed the edge of the gorge, unfortunately he bumped into a small tree which he grasped tightly while he felt around it with his feet, but alas there was just empty space. He was frightened to say the least, because he was likely to fall into the gorge, so he decided to hang onto the tree until first light. The only human beings within miles were some hunters looking for wild boars, and their voices soon ceased. There was no possible chance of being found, so he kept holding his tree with one hand, and massaged his body constantly to keep his blood circulating.

At first light he found little comfort because he was forced to make his way through virgin scrub land, wearing only one plimsole having lost the other one which was an absolute disaster. He finally made it back to his camper van covered in blood. With no one to help him he drove to the nearest telephone where he asked us for our assistance.

Hot drinks, a cooked breakfast and medical attention helped restore a very shaken Gerald into some normality. I told Daniel our neighbour, who was a hunt master and dog handler in one of the Ardeche hunting clubs, what had happened to Gerald. He said that anyone was lucky to survive a similar ordeal, because many people perish each year. It is always advisable to adventure off track with another person, and to leave a note of your whereabouts with a third person to be on the safe side.

Gerald was very grateful for our help in patching him up and restoring his morale, which was at an all time low. To show his appreciation of our hospitality over the years, he invited Faye, Alan and me to his Mayfair pad the next time we were back in the UK for our well-earned autumn holiday. He also invited my eldest daughter and her two sons to accompany him on a tour of some of his favourite tourist spots in London.

Gerald arranged for us to meet him in one of the well-known

clubs in the West End. Fortunately the taxi driver knew the exact location for there wasn't any highly polished brass plate to indicate the name of the club. I was surprised when the doorman was expecting us. We were to meet him in the Nash reception room, where Gerald was reading *The Times,* having eaten his porridge which was cooked especially for him every morning. We then followed him as he strode along the pavements, which I found were not paved with gold but led to the Overseas Club, where the Queen Mother was due to address the members. Faye and I were tickled pink to think that the red carpet was being laid for us.

We were not afforded the deference I expected from the waiter, because Gerald only ordered water for himself, but coffee for Faye, and he then asked which water was his preference. He replied that he only drank tap water, which was a real giveaway that he was hard up.

Our image of his Mayfair apartment was shattered when we were ushered into a small bedsitter in a church property, situated next to a park where we never heard a single nightingale sing a solitary note, all the time we were there. The one item which indicated that Gerald came from good stock was a painting of his father in his Admiral's uniform. We both were saddened to come to terms with the knowledge that he was reduced to living in a bedsitter and driving an old banger.

Nevertheless Gerald did his very best to entertain Faye and me, and the three other members of my family. He had gone to considerable lengths to introduce us to his way of life, and to find an itinerary which would suit the youngsters. We all appreciated the effort Gerald put in to make our outings a success, and it left us with some memorable moments getting to know what it is like living in Mayfair.

The following season Gerald left his camper van in our local garage in Saint Ambroix to be serviced, but he left it there until the following year. When he came to collect it the engine wouldn't start because he claimed that rats had chewed through the electric cables. To cut a story short, his behaviour was so violent that the garage owner called on the gendarmes to restrain him.

Later in the day Gerald arrived on our doorstep so disturbed that I couldn't reason with him. He wanted me to go to the garage and demand that the owner should rewire his old banger, and point out it was his rats that had done the damage, and as for the costs of garaging he could get lost. The realisation came that Gerald had advanced Alzheimer's disease that was the cause of his violent behaviour. I was not in a position to get involved, so I reluctantly declined to do as he demanded.

Some weeks later I was plastering one of the bedrooms on the second floor of the Mas, when I heard heavy feet stomping up the granite steps. Suddenly the door was flung open and in strode Gerald. It was only too obvious that he was in a very agitated state, and his words tumbled out of his mouth in a disorderly manner, but the gist of his meaning was that he wanted me to finance a visit to Marseille so that he could demand the British Consul to repatriate him back to the UK. Furthermore I was to pay for his hotel accommodation for his stay in Marseille.

It was at the time when Alan had fallen ill with cancer, Faye and I were unable to run our private hotel, and our cashflow was down to a dribble. Gerald became even more bad tempered than I could have imagined. The well of our hospitality and our bank accounts were nearly dried up, so he was out of luck. It was a very sad demise of our relationship with someone we had helped for so long.

9

Andorra la Vella

Alan's sister Judy was a regular visitor to our Mas who stayed for two-week breaks, two or three times a year, so she was very much part of the furniture. She enjoyed gardening and taking part in our social life, so it was agreed that all four of us would take a break, and on this occasion we decided to have a look at the Pyrenees, and stay in Andorra for two nights.

Andorra is an independent state squeezed between Spain and France, and I understood that Spanish was the predominant language. This would give Alan and his sister the opportunity to speak Spanish which they learned when they lived in Argentina for part of their childhood. We looked forward to enjoying seeing the majestic mountains and the ski slopes, and taking advantage of the duty free shopping.

Our first stopover was at Canet Plage, a modern sea side town which lacked the charm of the more popular resorts, and our hosts at our bed and breakfast accommodation were equally lacking in charm and welcome. Faye and Judy shared one room and Alan and I another one. Our hosts didn't even offer us a hot drink before we retired to bed.

In the middle of the night Alan and I were disturbed by Faye knocking on our door. She said that water was falling from the ceiling, and that they were both soaked as well as the bed. I would have to wake the owner and get him to find a alternative room. I knocked on the owner's door continuously until he asked me what was wrong. He refused to open his door. He didn't believe that his water pipes could possibly leak, and what did I expect him to do about it?

I replied that for a start an umbrella would be useful. My sarcasm prompted him to find a dry room, but the girls spent a miserable night. The atmosphere at breakfast was very unpleasant. There was no apology for the soaking, nor was any refund forthcoming. We were only too happy to get going.

The sunshine and the one hundred and thirty kilometre climb all the way to the Pas de la Case, which is about nine thousand feet above sea level, lightened our spirits no end. The only worry was a sound of a bearing running dry, and the radiator was heating up. It wasn't until I opened the window that I realised the screeching noise, which was getting louder and louder as we climbed, was caused by millions of large insects. I quickly closed the window in case we might find ourselves keeping company with the little beasts.

We reached the only petrol station, which is perched precariously on the mountainside, where I had once filled up in the middle of a snow storm in high summer. The snow was being blown upwards, and the strong wind gave me the feeling that I was going to be blown over the small parapet into oblivion. I hate to think what the winter weather is like at that altitude.

Good luck directed us to a modern hotel several kilometres outside the town of Andorra where the staff made us as welcome as best they could, because they only spoke their own language. We made ourselves at home in the bar enjoying the generous measures of our favourite drinks, when an Englishman introduced himself. One of the staff had telephoned him and suggested that he would enjoy our company. He most certainly hit it off with the four of us. Shortly afterwards Faye livened up every one in the bar by playing her mouth organ which put us all in the mood for some serious party going, which lasted until late in the evening. Our new friend was such good company we decided to invite him to an evening meal the following day at the hotel restaurant.

After a comfortable night and a prolonged breakfast, we pottered about enjoying the mountain scenery, until we stopped at a small bar for croissants and coffee. It wasn't long before a sad-looking Englishman asked if we minded him talking to us about his problem. It transpired that he had been seduced by a property firm which was offering free flights, transport and accommodation, so that prospective buyers could view properties in the Principality. He had recently divorced and the prospect of leading an entirely new life living in a superb apartment, fully furnished and close to the ski slopes, was exciting enough for him to sell up and buy his new lifestyle.

The reality of burning his boats consigned him to leading a miserable and lonely life, with little or no chance of selling up and returning to the UK. He was unable to speak the local language, and he found the English-speaking residents were not interested in befriending him. I felt guilty having enjoyed a happy and fulfilling life with our French neighbours and other friends. We were now leaving somebody who was considering buying a length of rope.

Our afternoon shopping turned out to be a damp squib, partly due to the lack of desirable goods which were within our means, and the depressing thoughts we still had concerning the lonely man we had met before lunch. However, our hunger for a decent meal with our guest soon turned our melancholy into anticipation of another memorable evening. The dinner was excellent and the wine provided by our guests was first class. Needless to say we spent the remainder of our evening at the bar.

Closing time was later than expected so we were rather tipsy when we all retired to our rooms, or so I thought, but where had Alan got to? A thorough search finally revealed him firmly locked in behind the glass door of the bar. He indicated that he had popped into the WC situated two floors down. The manageress hadn't checked that it was vacant, so she locked the hotel up for the night before crossing the road to the staff quarters.

Judy was the only one who could converse with the Spanish-speaking manageress, so she volunteered to get her to free Alan, who was no doubt considering helping himself to a drink to drown his sorrows. I remember Judy striding purposefully across the *route nationale*, towards the staff quarters, unaware in just her nightdress! She returned with the manageress and the key, but with the first signs of frostbite and embarrassment.

Our short holiday ended on a happy note which provided us with the opportunity of reminding her that she had been seen wandering about on a main road in Andorra past midnight. Pulling her leg at the critical moment after an evening meal with guests was guaranteed to raise an eyebrow and laughter.

10

Mai

The evening television news headline was the admission of the Duke of Edinburgh to the King Edward VII Hospital for Officers, with a chest infection. This was a precaution which was necessary because of his age. It was reported that his friend Joanna Lumley delivered flowers but did not visit HRH. This event brought back to mind the visit Faye and I made to one of the single wards, which are named after members of the royal family. It was a very sad occasion because our dearest friend Mai Zetterling was terminally ill and had asked us to visit her.

Rewinding my memory back to 1946, I recall sitting in the front row of the cinema in Llanelly south Wales when I was evacuated away from the dangers of flying bombs. I had spent my threepence pocket money to watch one of Mai Zetterling's early films. The film made me forget my loneliness as I sat there with no chance of seeing my parents until the war in Europe had ended.

Fast backwards now to 1985. Alan, Fay and I had purchased Le Mas Pradel. We were watching the world go by from the terrace of our favourite bar on market day in the comfort of the large bamboo chairs. Faye drew our attention to a woman walking towards us, carrying a very large basket filled with shopping, and wearing a garland of Spanish onions round her neck. She asked Faye if we lived locally or were we on holiday. Having established where we lived she invited us to a barbecue at her home, before trundling off towards her car. I did not expect to hear anything more about the invitation.

A few days later 'the onion woman' telephoned Faye and gave her instructions of how to find our way out into the sticks, where we

The notorious beautiful Russian spy found sanctuary at Le Mazel; seen here in Mai's kichen.

would find her home at the end of a very narrow and winding road. Faye then said, 'Are you by any chance Mai Zetterling?'

'Of course I am! How did you guess?' she replied.

We followed the narrow winding road which Mai had mentioned, but it came as a surprise to discover our friend owned the greater part of the hamlet of Le Mazel, which was a much more grandiose Mas than our Mas Pradel.

Louis her son was roasting a whole lamb for the barbecue to which the entire population of Le Mazel and the three of us had been invited. Our hostess obviously enjoyed the company of her guests, and we were to find that her many parties which we attended were a great success. Naturally Mai was always included in our own social life, although she was very picky when it came to choosing her company. She was always on the phone chatting to Faye about our latest guests, and I believe she was always on the lookout for suitable characters for her film scripts.

Towards the latter part of our time in Saint Ambroix, Mai tried hard to persuade Faye to dictate some of her memoirs of her time in Scotland and France. She found her stories had a great appeal. But our busy lives were fully occupied, renovating and running our private hotel.

One morning Mai arrived early enough to join us for lunch. However, that was not the reason for her visit. She explained that her numerous friends lived scattered in the four corners of the earth. She said that she had made up her mind to adopt Alan, Faye and me, as her family. We were flattered to think that Mai had taken a fancy to the three of us.

We soon discovered that Mai's live-in lover had departed, leaving her in a very vulnerable position, living alone with only two Irish wolfhounds and another hunting dog to keep her company, in an isolated spot, and in a house that had one of the exterior doors missing.

Alan and I soon fell for Mai's charms and her vulnerability, so off we went to secure her house and to do some minor repairs. Faye provided the shoulder for Mai to cry on during her very stressful time.

Not long after Mai's crisis Faye went down with a bad dose of flu, leaving our kitchen without the chef, and with an invalid who had taken to her bed. Much to my relief Mai's car came rattling down our long driveway, and out stepped Mai carrying her largest basket filled with all the ingredients necessary for the meals for us and our guests. She promptly told Alan and me to get lost because she preferred to run the kitchen and the cooking herself. Never in my wildest dreams, as a youngster watching *Only Two Can Play*, could I have imagined seeing the famous sexy bombshell washing up the dishes in our kitchen!

The actress and the bishop

Our advert in the *The Lady* magazine holiday section provided us with a regular supply of interesting guests, one of the most unusual of whom turned out to be a real live bishop whose church was in Amsterdam. We were not at all sure how to treat him, but we didn't need to stand on ceremony because he was very relaxed and normal.

His lively and humorous personality made him very popular with the staff and the other guests.

One day after the evening meal he was in a very mellow mood, having enjoyed Faye's cooking and the numerous glasses of our local wine. He confided in us that he and the other clergymen enjoyed drinking after the services down in the crypt. He of course had already drunk too much so he retired to his bedroom.

Well past midnight, when the Mas was silent enough to hear a pin drop, there was an almighty crash which woke me with a start. In my imagination it was God sounding J.A. Rank's gong to show his disapproval of the bishop encouraging his staff to drink after hours in the crypt.

Mai and Faye had their usual gossip about the guests, and sure enough Mai was fascinated by Faye's character reference about our Dutch bishop. She promptly invited the three of us and our interesting guests to a dinner party at Le Mazel. In my opinion it was just a cook-up to find character material for her writing.

The only lighting in her dining room was a huge black wrought iron candelabra, which was cleverly placed so that she could concentrate her attentions on her guest of honour. The aroma of Mai's cooking and the scent of the flowers put the final touch to the evening. After numerous glasses of Mai's favourite Tavel rosé wine, the conversation turned to Amsterdam, and the bishop mentioned where his church was situated. Mai knew the city well and said, 'Your church is in the red-light district, so you must be doing a good job there.'

The Bishop replied, 'I am sure you could do a better job there than I could.'

A visit to the vet

An early morning call from Le Mazel sounded urgent. One of Mai's dogs needed to have his wounds stitched as soon as possible. She had some how managed to get the dog into her car, but she needed help in taking the poor animal to the Saint Ambroix veterinary surgeon, as she was unable to manhandle it on her own. Faye asked me to accompany her to assist and translate if necessary. Mai, Faye and I waited for our turn to see the vet and attend the operation on the dog's lacerations.

Mai fancied the good-looking vet as he stitched up the wounds, and made some very flattering remarks to Faye about his good looks, hairstyle, and physique. She assumed he did not speak English, because he only responded to my French when he had the dog on the operating table, when he questioned Mai about the patient.

The poor dog was unconscious during and after the treatment, which included a strong dose of antibiotics. The vet then told Mai to be careful how she manhandled the dog into the car. Mai turned to Faye and said, 'Does he think I am a bloody Amazon?' The vet smiled at her remark and Mai blushed with embarrassment, as she remembered her flirtatious remarks. We returned to the Mas, leaving the dog still unconscious on the back seat of Mai's car.

We were all very relieved that all was well with the patient, so we retired to the kitchen for a well-deserved coffee and drop scones However, when Mai checked to see if the dog had regained consciousness, things were not at all as she expected. She found to her horror that the dog had messed his knickers, and the back seat of the car. Alan and I reluctantly played the part of perfect gentlemen and cleaned up the mess. Mai beat a hasty retreat, leaving behind her profuse apologies and an awful smell.

An hour or so later the telephone rang again from a very disturbed Mai. This time she said that Alan and I had overlooked a Churchillian-sized cigar shaped motion, which the dog had neatly arranged along the shelf on the dashboard, and another one carefully dropped inside her Gladstone-style handbag, on her make-up bag, and on her open purse.

Good friends are worth their weight in good deeds.

11

From the Sublime to the not so Sublime

Our three-star Cevennolle restaurant

During a committee meeting of The English Speaking Circle, I offered to organise a rally in the Cevennes for our members and their friends. This was an activity I was familiar with, having rallied at restricted and national events, and I had helped organise club rallies. Even the Sunday afternoon treasure hunt events needed to be carefully set up for safety reasons, and to ensure that the competitors did not get lost. The critical sections of the route are selected to test the driver and their navigator's skills, so small and tortuous roads in the Cevennes are ideal.

During my trial run Faye and I found ourselves in a tiny hamlet, surrounded by forests and close to a valley where a small road clung to one of its sides. I planned to use this hair-raising road to lead the cars back to civilisation. However, the breathtaking vistas more than compensated for the anxiety of falling over the edge, or finding the road was impassable.

It happened that our desire for something to eat and drink coincided with Faye spotting an ancient sign, which indicated that an uninspiring building had been a bar several generations ago. Faye had to encourage me to open the door because I thought the place was too run down. I did open the door, but to my surprise the room was furnished with ancient tables covered with faded oilcloth, and bench seats. There were several individual tables with genuine antique chairs to match.

I could hear signs of life coming from the kitchen. A few minutes later the cook appeared through the door and asked us what we would like. Warmed by her smile and our pleasant reception, we decided to stay a while, bask in the fascinating ambience, and enjoy our refreshments.

It transpired that this charming lady had kept her bar open every day of the previous thirty years. We often returned to enjoy the hospitality, and the homemade meals which were prepared from only local produce. We soon made friends with the family, and the husband asked us if we would like to have one of their dogs as a gift. We declined their kind offer as we already had two of our own, but told him that a close friend of ours was considering taking on a dog. Our friend Brian was delighted with the offer of the dog, so we introduced Brian and his wife Heather to our new friends. Both fell for the dog which remained joined at the hip with his new masters for the rest of his life.

We introduced another couple of our English Circle friends to our three-star restaurant, and they were equally fascinated with our choice of home cooking, and interesting countryside. The husband had planned to take his sister-in-law and her husband to the famous restaurant 'Maximes' in Paris, for a very special night out on the town. However, the Scottish brother in-law declined the invitation, so our friend decided to take them to our three-star family restaurant instead. These very wealthy folk had a memorable evening, eating good food, drinking fine local wine, and enjoying the good company of honest, friendly mountain folk. The event was a great success.

In the mire

Our seasonal flurry of guests had fully booked every single bed in the main building, and the two double beds in the renovated chicken house, which we fondly referred to as 'the cottage'. As usual Faye had made sure that everything was in order for the change-over. Fresh flowers had been arranged and the bottle of our local wine was ready for the first arrivals. However, the aroma was not from the flowers this time, and it was most unpleasant to say the least. This indicated that the septic tank needed emptying, but it was too late to hire anyone to empty the tank before our first guests arrived.

Armed with wellies, rubber gloves, shovels, a wheelbarrow and some

Brian, Alan and Faye's son, rendering the old chicken house

very bad language, Alan and I set to work removing loads of solids, and cleaning the filter tank. It was a desperate attempt to make sure that all four of our toilets would be working. Pits had to be dug close to our boundary to take the waste material, and the grass carefully replaced to conceal what we had been doing in the disused field.

Unfortunately the pipe system, which allowed the filtered liquid to drain into the huge pit, was completely blocked by the roots of a willow tree which had been planted in order to get rid of some of the waste liquid. To dispose of the liquid I contrived to divert the outfall into the field, but the pipework was buried and the turfs carefully replaced.

Prior to the arrival of our paying guests, we had an unexpected visit from two curious visitors who always asked questions about our property. It made them even more curious, because it was unlike Alan and me to be outside in wellies, with yellow gloves on, when the temperature was 39 degrees centigrade, and the shade of our acacia trees and cool drinks beckoned our sweat-drenched bodies away from our hard labour.

Our mammoth task was well worthwhile, because without the use of the four toilets we would have been obliged to pay for alternative accommodation for everyone who had booked their holiday with us. The following week the largest tanker managed to clean and empty the septic tank, and the remainder of our time in Le Mas Pradel was trouble free. Only the strange rectangular lush green patches in the field were there to remind us, and the owner of the field how we had averted being up to our armpits in s✱✱t.

12

Yoko and Jacqueline

Faye, Alan and I had joined The English Circle, which held its monthly meetings every Thursday in Alès, except for the summer season. Yoko, an American of Finnish origin, and his French wife Jacqueline made us feel very much at home the first time we attended a Thursday meeting.

Within a few weeks we had been invited to their farmhouse, which Yoko was extending and modernising. Unfortunately he did not get on very well with his various builders, so either he lacked the finance to complete his project, or the tradesmen could not stand being told by a well-known American architect how to do their jobs.

Yoko playing his beloved violin

Time passed very quickly because we were up to our eyes in our own renovation work, and taking in paying guests. However, we managed to keep up our two-way social lives. Jacqueline proved to be an excellent hostess and by nature a genteel lady. Yoko loved playing jazz on his violin and Alan also played violin, piano and organ. Faye also played the organ, accordion and piano and we all enjoyed our musical evenings.

Gradually Yoko became rather more eccentric than he had been when we had first met him. Faye's medical knowledge, and her years spent in nursing, had earned her the reputation of being 'the best doctor in town'. I suspect that she had already diagnosed Alzheimer's disease as being the cause of his worrying behaviour. Mary Poppins and her lame ducks was another good title, which Faye had also deserved because she always made sure anybody in trouble would be looked after no matter what the cost, and she was very adept at organising other people to help her lame ducks.

Latterly Yoko became violent and Faye threatened him that she would seek help from the police if he continued to distress his wife. Eventually Jacqueline was found injured in the toilet, and she remained seriously ill and disturbed for the rest of her life. She was moved to six different clinics and hospitals without anybody being able to diagnose the cause of her condition. Finally she was moved to the hospice in our town, so she would be near dear Faye and her English friends.

One evening meal we were enjoying the company of some lively friends when we received a telephone call from one of the hospitals in Nimes. The nightshift caretaker explained that a Mr Hakola had visited his wife but had forgotten where he had parked his car. He had mislaid his wallet and had been without anything to eat or drink all day, and he was unable to pay for his fare back home. Our telephone number was the only one he could remember, so we were called upon to rescue Yoko once more.

Alan admirably held the fort whilst Faye and I drove to the hospital at Nimes. Yoko's greeting was not what we expected. 'What on earth are you doing here?' This left me dumbfounded because he seemed to be on a different planet, and his conversation with the caretaker didn't make sense. Faye insisted that we should find somewhere to feed and water him, so we managed to scrape together enough francs for a modest meal for Yoko and strong coffees for the three of us. We returned our friend safely to his home in Alès then we returned to join Alan and our guests. Alas only the leftovers remained to feast upon!

Whatever Yoko's relationship with his wife had been latterly, he missed her good cooking and her company. He made a habit of calling at the Mas just before Faye served the evening meal, knowing that Faye would never refuse a visitor something to eat, and she would quickly lay an extra place setting so he could enjoy a proper meal and some company, before returning to his empty house.

In spite of Yoko losing the plot when it came to dealing with everyday problems, he could play jazz on his violin and create superb paintings. It was very sad for us to rescue him from the consequences of his illness.

On one occasion a phone call from the Alès hospital, where his wife was being treated, urgently requested Faye's assistance in dealing with Yoko, who imagined that he was being interrogated by the Sécurité (MI6), whereas the administrator was only trying to fill in a necessary form concerning his wife's income and her social security position. We arrived post haste, and as we walked towards the office, Yoko's ravings could be heard reverberating along the corridor. Inside the office were numerous white-coated members of staff with their backs to the wall, while Yoko held them petrified by his threats and ravings.

Faye confronted Yoko with a few well-chosen words which quietened him down, as if by magic. It transpired that he thought the secret service was spying on him, and he had made up his mind that he would not give them any information whatsoever, even if they tortured him! He was also upset that his wife had been moved to the psychiatric wing of the hospital.

We returned home very concerned at the turn of events, and Faye decided to seek professional advice about the patient's condition, from a consultant from a well-known London hospital who was staying with us. Faye told him that she believed the problem had been caused by Jacqueline's family doctor, who had stopped one of her drugs which was essential for her wellbeing, and that she was physically ill and not a mental case. Our guest contacted the hospital the following day, and conveyed his opinion that the patient should not be in a psychiatric ward. Jacqueline was returned to the general hospital on our guest's advice.

Not long after Jacqueline had been found injured and unconscious in the WC. she was taken to a hospital in Montpellier. Faye suggested she and I should accompany Yoko in his car to visit her, as he was unable to cope with journey on his own. All went well for the first few kilometres until Faye asked Yoko what actually happened to his wife in the WC.

I forget the actual words of abuse which preceded him losing his temper completely. I was sitting behind Yoko as he swung the steering wheel hard over, and headed directly towards a fast oncoming articulated vehicle. I dived over the front seat, wrenched the steering wheel from his hands and managed to steer us to safety. I applied the handbrake hard enough to bring the car to a halt in spite of Yoko still keeping his foot on the accelerator. I refused to let him drive as I feared for our lives. Jacqueline was in intensive care when we arrived at the hospital, but it seemed that her condition had not been resolved.

Her youngest son Antonni, who lived in America, came to sort out his parents' affairs, but he had an almost impossible task because his father turned against him and reduced him to tears on occasions. However, the court had the common sense to give Antonni the power of attorney over his parents. Faye, Alan and I regarded the poor lad as our adopted son during the relocation of his father to an old folks' village in America where he was looked after by professional staff. Jacqueline remained in our local hospice. Faye visited her frequently and was offered a job on the staff as she had cheered up so many of the old ladies. I once saw her being grabbed round the waist by the male nurse, who then whisked her down the corridor to the amusement of the patients. Jacqueline did not die alone and the nuns blessed Faye for being such a stalwart friend.

We three assisted in helping Antonni sell up his parents' home, before returning to America where he looked after both his troublesome brother and his father. The good news was that Antonni finally met his soulmate. He richly deserved a happy life for being a loving and caring son.

13

The Long Journey

Faye and Alan's youngest son Brian had decided that he and his partner and their daughter would leave France and return to the Isle of Eigg in the Inner Hebrides, where they had lived prior to Brian working for Mai Zetterling. Faye was anxious that Brian took the opportunity to load up his Renault 14 with many useful items, to help him set up their family home again. By the time he was ready to leave, the car was fully loaded and the roof rack was not designed to take the weight it was carrying.

Brian looked very unsure of himself having to cope with a 1,500-kilometre journey in an unstable car, and the chance of a breakdown. I volunteered to accompany him as a relief driver and mechanic. From then onwards the die was cast, because he needed to be back on the island within three days.

Our hurried departure from Saint Ambroix did not leave us time to check the current road and traffic conditions. In any event the weather was set dry and sunny for the foreseeable future, so we set off in high spirits. The first 72 kilometres to Pont Saint Esprit left me feeling that the car was seriously overloaded, and Brian was finding it hard keeping it stable on the bends. There was no plan B for ditching some excess weight, or cancelling the trip, so Brian pressed on towards the Autoroute du Soleil.

When we reached the N7 I was horrified to see the entire northbound and southbound lanes were completely jammed as far as the eye could see. We drove 4 kilometres further on hoping to join the Autoroute du Soleil and head north. Alas! All the traffic had come to a standstill in both directions. A gendarme told us that the national strike had virtually made it impossible for us to reach Calais.

Brian looked so downcast I suggested that I could navigate our way on minor roads all the way to the coast, providing that he was game to do all the driving. Having competed in three national 'navigator nightmare' rallies, I felt confident I could keep us travelling towards Calais without encountering the pickets.

Hour after hour we maintained our routine, and we were rewarded by seeing superb scenery unfold as we negotiated some very small and winding lanes. The only problem was, we did not come across any bars or restaurants, as we were obliged to avoid even the villages. I was beginning to feel self assured about my navigational prowess at avoiding the road blocks. However, it was only by chance we did not get stuck in a road block, because a gentleman flagged a coach down and explained to the driver and to me how to avoid the road block ahead.

The small lane was barely wide enough, and the last we saw of the coach was stuck in a farm yard. A very large lorry preceded us downhill through some woods, scattering the branches as though a giant hedge trimmer was at work. The lane eventually joined a wide road which bypassed the road block. Once again we were back to our tiring routine.

Bypassing Lyon was a feather in our caps, and we had enough feathers in our caps for us to fly past Dijon.

The strikers obviously had no intention of picketing during the night and losing their sleep. We must have joined the autoroute to Calais via Reims, just before the flood gates opened and the backlog of thousands of irate drivers joined the rush to complete their journeys. For the first time since we started to drive on the minor roads, Brian was able to keep his foot firmly on the accelerator, where it remained for the five hundred and twenty four kilometres to Calais, because the autoroute was completely empty all the way.

The channel crossing gave us some well-deserved rest, and a chance to rehydrate ourselves with several cups of delicious tea, and fill our stomachs with some doubtful pastries. Brian and I went our separate ways once we reached London: he continued on towards Eigg, and I booked my ticket at Waterloo station to Avignon. I managed to replenish my empty stomach again, before starting the longest rail journey imaginable.

THE LONG JOURNEY

Travellers had been warned that the French national strike was causing utter chaos on both the railways and the roads, so long delays could be expected. However, the journey to Boulogne passed without a hitch, although the passengers were very anxious because the gossip indicated that we might not find a train waiting for us when our ferry docked. The good news was finding a train waiting for us at the terminus, but the bad news was it could not make up its mind if it was going to Paris, or remaining glued to the railway lines.

Eventually a non-union driver appeared, and to our relief he decided to make for Paris. After several unexplained stops en route we arrived in Paris, where I used the metro to reach the next station where a train was probably going to take me to Avignon. The train was waiting for the crowd of very worried-looking passengers like myself to climb aboard. Surprise surprise, it started on time and headed south through the moonless night. The other passengers in my compartment started discussing the likelihood of us reaching our destinations, because of the unexpected stops and delays which kept interrupting the journey.

Rumours soon spread from one compartment to another, that the strikers had resorted to blocking the tracks with railway sleepers and anything else they could find. However, the train continued on its way with more stoppages, until we finally came to a halt some one hundred or so kilometres north of Lyons, where we waited for daylight to find that we had come to a halt at a small town station. Everybody was expecting to have news about the strike, and how it was going to affect our chance of getting home. Someone on board had a radio and spread the bad news that our track was blocked, and if it was lifted we would have to change to another train which was parked up on the other platform.

Throughout the hot sunny day we had no further information about the strike and our predicament. The mayor declared an emergency, because we had been without anything to drink or eat, and there was every chance that we would dehydrate in the high temperatures inside the train. The local volunteers provided some modest food, bottled water and cups of very welcome tea. There was no possibility at all that the train would go anywhere. I decided to persuade the three other passengers to share a taxi with me, so that we could reach

Lyon and avoid the blockage. Alas, none of the taxi drivers were willing to leave the town, because the petrol stations were closed in sympathy with the strikers and they did not want to run out of fuel.

Frustration, bad temper, and exhaustion were widespread, so the mayor called upon the riot police to keep a presence in the station, in case we all rioted. However, late that evening a rumour spread like wildfire that the train parked on the other track was about to take us on our way. Many passengers like myself gathered up their luggage and changed over to the other train. Fortunately the passengers who had not moved started to shout and gesticulate that we had got on the wrong train, and that their one was about to leave. I threw caution, myself, and my bags out of the carriage and onto the tracks, and a thoughtful man opened his carriage door and hauled me and my gear on board, just as the train started to leave.

My last view of the station as we pulled away was of the large piles of excreta where the train's WCs had been situated for so long. Every passenger on board must have been relieved to smell the sweet night air, and to be on the move at last.

Long before we reached Avignon the train was diverted onto an unused track to avoid another blockage on the main line. The train progressed at an excruciatingly slow pace, as it swayed from side to side pushing its way through the overhanging foliage.

I finally reached Avignon, where I found an obliging taxi driver who was prepared to drive me home just as he was about to go home to his bed. Without this man's kindness I would have spent another night sleeping rough. Having spent the best part of three days losing weight and being bored out of my mind, returning to Le Mas Pradel and my friends was pure heaven.

14

Habits and Customs

Car parking

The first time I paid attention to the problem of car parking in Saint Ambroix I was sitting outside our favourite cafe opposite the town square, enjoying watching the world go by with Alan and Faye. We noticed a local driver who found his car wedged in so tightly that he couldn't extricate it. He glanced up and down the street hoping to see if the owners of these cars were returning. He waited for a while before getting into his car and then started his engine. To our amazement he began ramming the car in front, and then rammed the one behind. Having repeated the process he managed to make enough room for him to drive away, without anyone reprimanding the escapee for damaging the two cars!

One of our wealthy French friends drove 'a deux chevaux' for his everyday visits for shopping in Alès where he lived, but for longer or more important journeys he used his upmarket, top of the range Citroen shooting brake. When I pulled his leg about driving an old banger, he said that it was in excellent condition, it was cheap to run and there was no vehicle licence fee, and furthermore he couldn't care a damn if his car accumulated a few dents and scratches whilst parking.

Even the German Chancellor used a well worn VW for his mistress to go shopping from his hide-away near Saint Ambroix.

Daniel, our neighbour and Chief of the Municipal Police, explained how he coped with the bad parkers. The first infringement would be dealt with by simply pointing out the drivers had parked incorrectly. The second offence would merit an official warning, and the third offence would be a fine.

Most French drivers have a very casual attitude towards parking regulations, even when they are abroad. I remember having dinner in a French restaurant in Brighton, when a Frenchman was trying to impress his girlfriend. The restaurant owner had politely told him that his car was most probably going to be towed away, because he was parked on a double yellow line. The man made it very clear in a loud voice that he had no intention of moving his car.

An hour or so later, when the couple were enjoying their coffees and brandies, the sound of the recovery vehicle winching their posh car on board put a damper on the Frenchman's ardour at the prospect of being without his passion-wagon. I did wonder if the restaurant owner had taken his revenge and telephoned the vehicle recovery company!

The owner of a medical laboratory in Ales became exasperated when he found someone was using his private car park without his permission, and one day he found the same car was parked in his own reserved space. Drastic measures were called for to stop this ever happening again. He turned up for work the following day in his four-by-four instead of his usual saloon. The busy road in front of the laboratory was part of a one-way system, where all vehicles were prohibited from parking. He hitched his powerful four-by-four to the offending car and dragged it into the middle of the road, successfully causing complete deadlock throughout the town centre.

The magistrate who presided over the case must have had a good sense of humour and justice, because he fined the owner of the offending vehicle, and added points to his driving licence. If this incident had taken place in the UK it would have been the owner of the four-by-four who would have received the fine and points to his licence.

A Dutch university tutor, who had given up his lifestyle to be a pig farmer, invited the three of us to visit his home and to meet his English wife and family. We had something in common because at one time he had owned Les Volets Rouge, and this coincidence led us to buy Le Mas Pradel. We were anxious to get to know what they had found it like living in France on the top of a small mountain.

The access to the farm was via a narrow road and the only place to park was where the road was wide enough for vehicles to pass one another, so I parked up and we went the rest of the way on foot, which included climbing a steep ancient path. Our visit proved to be most interesting, and Gus and his wife made us very welcome. In fact we have remained firm friends to this very day.

The telephone rang and everything changed, because a neighbour had threatened to tip my car down the mountainside with his forklift truck, if I didn't move it immediately. Our hosts were very upset at the turn of events, and explained that the man was prone to violent tempers.

A year or so later the neighbour went berserk and threatened to kill his wife with his woodcutter's axe. Fortunately someone called the gendarmes, and they quickly surrounded the house. The lunatic's doctor was also called out, and was given the option of talking some sense into his patient. The other option was that they would shoot him.

We never found out what was the outcome of this incident, because the man was never heard of again, although I presume he retired to a mental asylum. I often wondered what would have happened that day if I hadn't moved my car. Perhaps he would have used his axe in preference to the forklift truck!

La chasse

At the age of sixteen my best friend Trevor invited my brother Norman and me to visit his relations, who lived on the smallest of the seven hills of Malvern. We all owned motorcycles and we had a great time touring together. However, Trevor's uncle decided we would all enjoy hunting rabbits on his neighbour's farmland, armed with his small shotgun, which necessitated stalking the prey and getting as close as possible in order to make a clean kill.

When it came to my last turn with the shotgun, I spotted a rabbit well out of range, but well downhill. I was surprised to see my prey fall over, but it was certainly still alive and kicking. I was told in no uncertain manner that I should not have attempted to make a kill out of range. I was told to run after the poor creature and break its neck to put it out of its misery. The look on the rabbit's face made me despise myself for being unnecessarily cruel, for the sake of a few moments of excitement. My feelings remained with me during my life in France where the hunt for wild boar is so popular. Our neighbour was the hunt master and responsible for keeping the huge dogs which are capable of killing the boar themselves.

Late one evening we heard one of the boars crying in pain somewhere near the Mas on the rocky hillside in front of us, not more than several hundreds of metres from our front door. One of the hunters had been unable to get near enough to kill the boar. Many hours later during the night, the crying ceased, leaving the entire household to cope with their nightmares.

Daniel our neighbour, being the hunt master for one of the Ardèche hunts, was responsible for keeping the pack of hunting dogs, and they were often kept down the end of our private lane in his kennels. One year his favourite dog won an international award at a show in Spain, and naturally Daniel was very proud of his pet hunting dog. However, once Daniel forgot to keep his routine for letting the pack jump into his van, which was to let his pet, the leader of the pack, to be the first to jump in. His pet suddenly became a killing machine and savaged his master so badly he was kept in hospital for weeks while he was patched up and filled with countless antibiotics.

Several years later he showed the best of his pack at the local dog show, and invited us to visit the show and see his latest show stopper, a magnificent powerful hunting dog. Alan, Faye and I decided to take a constitutional walk into town to have a look at Daniel's pride of his pack. As we approached the dog pen Daniel was overheard to say to his police colleague that Jasper our border terrier was not at all frightened of his dog, who was capable of killing a boar himself. Daniel opened the pen and Jasper walked round the monster and raised his head before casually turning away.

Jasper's breed is unknown in France, so he drew lots of attention wherever we went. Stories of Jasper's courage and intelligence make interesting reading and Jaspers 2 and 3 all have displayed the same fine traits.

I always imagined that the hunt members spent their time stalking their prey in the woods, but in reality it is the hunt master who spends lots of time before the hunt, using his dogs to trace the scent

HABITS AND CUSTOMS

of the boars, so that on the day of the hunt the master can make his pack drive the boar that has been selected towards the waiting members, who have the opportunity to make the kill. It takes a well-placed single shot to make a clean kill. To see the club members often placed along a public road, waiting for ages just for the chance to fire a single shot, seems to be an unsuitable pastime for some of the elderly members who imagine they are still brave young hunters, instead of being arthritic pensioners. The first day of the hunting season, it is often said that there are more mothers-in-law who are accidentally shot than the wild boars.

Sadly there are many sadistic and unscrupulous hunters who come from the cities up north, who will stop at nothing to get their prey, even if they set fire to the woodland and scrubland to make it easy to find the boars when the land is opened up. One year arsonists placed oil drums in their hunting ground, some few miles north of our Mas. They set light to them one after another, and within hours the forest was ablaze, which created the greatest natural disaster in Europe. Alan and I considered that the Mas might be threatened because the smoke was already above the building.

We thought it prudent to see for ourselves if we might have to leave the Mas. The sight of the fire was in no way less frightening than the Australian bushfires shown on TV. Many of the fires we experienced during our time in Saint Ambroix were indeed awesome, and I could only wonder at the courage of the firefighters, who worked continuously in incredible heat and constant danger. The voluntary pilots who waterbombed the buildings, and other important fire fronts, have to take their life in their hands, as they often need to fly too close to make their precious water snuff out the fires. On one occasion the aircraft had to fly just above our Mas, then cross the roofs of the houses with only metres to spare, so that the water dropped exactly where it was needed. Many brave pilots have lost their lives over the years.

Our friend Gus the pig farmer, who lived in isolation surrounded by woods, was rescued by a waterbomber which dropped water on the farmhouse, damaging the roofs but saving the lives of the family.

15

The Bazalgettes and Andrew

The house without bedrooms

A house agent knocked on the door of our friends Jack and Jo Bazalgette's house and asked them if the rumour was true, that they had built their new house without any bedrooms. 'Yes,' Jack replied, 'we did not need them because we use our large motor home to sleep in.'

This remarkable couple found the prospect of retiring was alien, having worked and travelled widely helping refugees, and also working in the field of child care for Barnardo's. Their time in India, where Jack was a political officer prior to the British withdrawal, was hard to replicate in England.

Eventually they settled down about a half an hour's drive from Le Mas Pradel, when they purchased a large plot of land and built their home, which contained all the facilities needed for themselves and their family who would use the land as a family campsite.

Fay, Alan and I found Jack and Jo's company most rewarding, because Alan had been a deputy manager of a tea plantation in India at the age of twenty-two, and later served as a captain in the army during the Second World War both in India and Burma, so Alan and Jack had a lot in common. The three of us enjoyed visiting our new friends, and likewise Jack and Jo enjoyed our parties where the English Circle members and our other friends got together. Our Christmas Day event usually included them if their family was unable to join them. Our dining room was always packed to the ceiling each memorable Christmas and it was great fun. Their daughter Evelyn continues the family tradition of helping others, and she still

Christmas with friends

advises the World Bank and other charitable organisations on the needs of developing countries, and how to ensure that the finance can be put to the very best possible use. To this end she lives amongst the people to assess their needs. She has even helped women start their own enterprises where they have never had the freedom before of handling money. The emancipation of women in many of the African countries has been encouraged by the work of people like Evelyn Bazalgette.

Another well-known ancestor of theirs was the famous engineer who designed the London sewerage system, which cured the 'Great Stink'. This project was one of the most important engineering projects of its time and is still responsible for the improvement in the health of Londoners, and the sweeter smell of the Thames.

Gradually Jack's health declined enough to ring alarm bells, so the house without bedrooms was extended, with bedrooms, a stairlift, and a library, to replace their much-loved motor home which was called 'The Cuckoo'. Jack's last Christmas Day was spent with our 'Christmas Crowd', and his wife and daughter. Faye, Alan and I had been in the habit of inviting our friends who were without their family or any company for Christmas Day. Jack joined us for the dinner and he joined in the celebrations as though nothing was amiss, until Faye and I helped him onto the bed in the room next to the dining room for a rest.

Looking back to the time we three joined the English Circle, it was Jack and Jo who stepped forward and extended the hands of friendship. Our happy lives in France were guaranteed at this first meeting, where we began to forge our good relationships with the members.

Andrew

Faye was wandering round our local supermarket one day when she noticed a typical male English tourist who was obviously shopping just for himself, and he certainly looked very lonely. She decided to ask him if he was English. 'I most certainly am not,' he replied. 'I am Scottish,' he added in an offhand manner. This did not put Faye off, and she managed to find out that he had bought a house in an old coal mining village where we had rented Les Volets Rouge during our search for a new home. This gave her something in common and it was the start of our friendship.

Andrew had rejected a suburban life in England, and had made his home in a caravan which he dragged around the south of France behind a large Jaguar car. Eventually he decided to buy a building which had been three apartments for coal miners before the pit was closed. It took him nearly eight years to complete the renovation of the property.

Unfortunately his income consisted of a disability allowance and a very modest pension, which was not enough to live on and to restore his property. Nevertheless he was too proud to accept any offers of loans or gifts of some ready cash, when he was getting desperate for food. On one occasion we had to insist that he accepted enough for emergency phone calls. Another time he had to return to the UK to sort out a problem with his disability allowance, which left him without any money to pay for the fare. Fortunately the three of us were about to leave for our autumn holiday in Bexhill, so he reached

Dover at no cost at all. We offered to treat him to a lunch but he declined, making some feeble excuse. We later discovered that he just had enough cash to pay for his fare to Blackheath where he was going to stay with his mother, but he had been without anything to eat during our journey.

After he returned to France, Faye said that we could spare one of our carpets, to make his home more comfortable and warmer during the cold winter. Andrew was delighted with his carpet and he asked me to thank Faye and Alan for their gift. I discovered to my embarrassment that I had given away their best Indian carpet, which Faye had planned to lay in our posh salon. Nevertheless Andrew was pleased with the substituted carpet. Over the following years we got to know him very well and we included him in our circle of friends.

Andrew was in fact a Doctor of Philosophy, who devoted many years studying the world's religions, and he became a missionary in New Guinea, where he lived among the natives. He recounted many strange happenings which occurred during his time spent a million miles away from civilisation. At one stage of his time in the jungle, he decided to live on a beach where access was only possible by canoe and several days trekking from the nearest human beings. He wished to philosophise and come to some conclusions about his knowledge of all the various religions he had studied.

He had carefully arranged some netting inside his tent to prevent any of the dangerous insects from dropping on him whilst he slept. One night a flesh-eating wasp landed on his leg, and before he could pluck up courage it had eaten its way right down to the bone. How he survived the infection of his wound he put down to God's will. After that event he spent time with natives who had little if any contact with the outside world. The villagers gathered together whenever any important problem arose, which was like a village council meeting. The only problem on the agenda was the river which had changed its course over the years, and it was so far from the village that the women complained it took too long to collect the water. After many hours of deliberations it was decided that the river should change its course so that they could stay put. Having closed the meeting everyone went home to bed. At first light Andrew was astounded to find that the river had been conveniently redirected closer to the village!

Andrew experienced other strange happenings, which to Westerners were unbelievable. However, he assured me that he only recounted the truth, although the following incident stretched my imagination to the limit.

He was very anxious to visit another part of the countryside which he thought was only a couple of days walk through the forest, to what seemed to be a very interesting area with no obvious tracks or even small paths marked on his map. He asked the Headman if there were any paths he could follow to his destination. The Headman was emphatic in his reply, that it was impossible for him to find his way through the dense forest where many dangers awaited the foolhardy. He did however offer to take him there, providing he closed his eyes and stood still. Andrew did as he was told and after a while he opened his eyes. Behold, he was standing on a hilltop looking down on a completely new panoramic scene, which resembled what he would have expected if he had actually visited his destination. He stood there bewitched by this strange experience, which eventually faded away and once more he returned to the village. He naturally asked the Headman what had occurred and how he had made him visit his destination, but he declined to comment.

At a tea party one day with our friends we were introduced to a government officer who had been stationed in the same country, who recounted several experiences which confirmed Andrew had in fact told us true stories about the natives.

16

Disaster on the Route Nationale 110

During our time in France, Le Mas Pradel became a refuge for English residents and holidaymakers who had need of Faye's medical expertise, her advice, or our practical help. So it was not unusual for us to cope with telephone calls asking for our help. This time it was a call from the Alès hospital, to tell us there had been a major accident on the N110 route some 13 miles from Alès. Their request for us to assist them was quickly agreed, and then we were told that a coachload of teenage English school pupils had been seriously injured when their coach left the road on a bend, leaving everyone injured, including ten who had already died. We were asked to make ourselves available to comfort the parents of the pupils, who would be arriving at the Alès hospital late that evening. Our specific task was to remain on duty in the morgue, and escort the parents of the deceased, so that they could relate to sympathetic English people as they visited their loved ones for the last time.

The authorities in England had chartered an aircraft to fly the parents to Nimes airport, and coaches brought them to Alès hospital and other hospitals where the injured were being operated on. The British Consul and his wife joined the support staff and Faye and me, for a meeting to discuss the arrangements for the parents during their visit to the hospital, and for their accommodation which was being paid for by the Mayor of Alès, on behalf of the people of the town.

Faye pointed out that everything was being done for the children, but no thought was being given for the parents' wellbeing, after such a devastating shock of finding that their children had been either injured or had already died. The Consul's wife asked what Faye had in mind, to which she replied, 'At least a cup of tea and something to eat would be a good start.'

Within twelve hours after the accident the parents had been traced and notified of the accident, also every parent had arrived at the hospital. I regard this as a masterpiece of organisation. The bodies of the teenagers were beautifully prepared as though they were sleeping peacefully.

My own inadequate words cannot express my feelings for the distressed parents as they stood beside their loved ones. Faye coped like the professional nurse and gentle soul she is. The father of one of the unfortunate girls was alone for some reason, and was in such a distressed state because he had no religion to support him in his grief. Faye's gentle approach encouraged him to seek solace in the chapel. We happened to notice him on our way past the chapel, praying on his knees. We returned home during the night emotionally drained, and exhausted by the experience.

The next call from the hospital was for Faye and me to sort out some problems for a young Englishman who had taken off on his motorcycle, without telling his parents that he was in France. Unfortunately he had been involved in a nasty accident which left him with broken bones and no money to pay for his treatment. The poor lad was finding it difficult to make himself understood by some of the staff, but he was told that two English hospital helpers would be able to contact his parents for him. The most important thing to do was to let his parents know what had happened to their son, that he was being cared for in hospital, and that he was expected to recover without any permanent damage.

17

Our Paying Guests

Taking bookings for our paying guests could sometimes bring surprises, because we knew so little about them before they arrived. We had been fortunate in choosing a suitable magazine to advertise our accommodation, as it produced an excellent supply of interesting and pleasant clients. Only two of these bookings gave us any serious concern during the time we were in business.

It all happened when two Irish families booked a week's holiday at the same time: one rented the cottage, and the other one stayed in the Mas itself for half board and lodging. Both families had two teenage children, and everyone seemed to be enjoying their holiday in the sunshine.

Faye had the bright idea that the youngsters would enjoy themselves if they went to the town festival together, where they could enjoy modern music and dancing in the market place. The parents would then be free to enjoy traditional music and dancing for the older generation in the town square. Faye assured the parents that their youngsters would come to no harm, as bad behaviour was unheard of in Saint Ambroix.

Faye's suggestions went down like a lead balloon, when the father who was staying in the Mas suddenly said, 'We don't have anything to do with those in the cottage.' It dawned on us all that we had booked a Catholic family in the Mas and a Protestant family in the cottage.

The morning temperature was already rising towards thirty eight degrees centigrade, but the atmosphere between the two groups began to change from polite to hostile. We were also subjected to his opinions about the English, which verged on little more than ravings of a bigot. It was such a disappointment that both families lost a great opportunity to continue enjoying themselves, and reach some understanding and sympathy for the other sides of the Northern Ireland troubles.

One of the very rare single bookings turned out to be a very elderly gentleman, who had visited the south of France with his wife and her best friend the previous year touring in his own car. He had been very taken with our part of France, but had his holiday spoiled by the constant instructions which the two passengers made thoughout the tour. When it came to planning the next summer holiday, he informed his wife that he was going to spend his week's holiday at Le Mas Pradel on his own.

We were very surprised to see an elderly man step out of his car, which was laden with camping gear which he had used at various campsites on the way south. We need not have worried that he would find it difficult to fit in with our other guests, or to find things to do with his afternoons. One of the guests, a bit of a comedian, found him parked up on the roadside in one of our beauty spots fast asleep. He banged on the car roof and demanded in French that he move his vehicle. The man awoke with a start and made his apologies, before he realised someone was pulling his leg. However, he made himself very much at home with us, and we were sad when the time came for him to leave.

Faye was surprised when he offered her a substantial tip, and a set of small serving pans, when he was settling his account. She took the opportunity to ask how he had found his holiday with us. His reply, 'It was better than I expected,' made Faye burst out laughing. She thanked him for his generosity and returned the tip which she said was not necessary, because we had all enjoyed his company.

A week later the three of us set off for our annual autumn holiday, and had boarded the cross channel ferry to Dover when we met our guest in the cafeteria. 'My God,' he said, 'my wife will raise merry hell when I phone and tell her that I am bringing my attractive landlady with me!'

Over the years we made many good friends with our guests, like Hal when he arrived with his son and his girlfriend. We soon discovered that his wife had died, leaving him griefstricken, so his son had planned to take his father and girlfriend on holiday to help him recover from his loss. We were in the habit of joining our guests after their evening meal if they invited us to join them for a coffee and a chat. Faye asked the couples who were in the dining room where they first met one another.

Hal's son turned to his girlfriend and said, 'We met at Broadmoor.' That must be one of the best conversation stoppers I have ever heard. The letdown was that they were both psychoanalysts. We have kept in touch with Hal, and he tells us that his son is now a well-known professor, and he and his wife still have fond memories of their holiday at Le Mas Pradel where their twins were conceived.

Faye completely forgot on one occasion that she had advertised in a local newspaper in England, which did not produce any takers for our accommodation, so it came as a surprise when she received a call which sounded like one of her friends pulling her leg. This led to some confusion, which finally confirmed a booking for two brothers for a week in the hottest time of the year. However, the caller was very anxious to find out if our rooms had en suite facilities. He was very surprised to hear that our rambling old Mas only had two bathrooms and one cloakroom.

Peter booked the remaining room for himself and his brother, because they seldom managed to spend any quality time together, so they intended to make the most of their holiday at Le Mas Pradel. It did not take long to learn that Peter was a major in the Irish Rangers, and his brother modestly said that he was a coalman. I should add that he bought and sold his stock by the ship-load.

This pair were on the go morning, noon and night, and managed to do more in a week than most of our guests did in a fortnight. They rounded up most days with a serious drinking session on our upper terrace, where they invited anyone who had enough stamina to keep going to the early hours. One of their evening sessions was with Brian, Faye and Alan's son, at the Mazel which was Mai Zetterling's huge Mas where Brian was the caretaker and her carer. It was a memorable party in which our two brothers enjoyed everything except their hangovers.

Faye was a thoughtful patron of our private hotel, and she took her responsibilities towards her guests very seriously. She always made

The author and Faye's son, Brian; the Ardèche

sure that the guests were made aware of the midday temperatures, which reached 41.5 degrees centigrade, in the shade of our acacia trees. Such high temperatures can kill the elderly and young alike if they don't cover up and avoid the sun between twelve and four.

Our two hardy brothers set off the next day to canoe down the Ardèche river, with its outstanding gorge and many rapids. It was an experience which Brian, my own son Paul and I had completed and found it tiring and very hot work, but great fun.

Peter had naturally been hardened to extreme conditions being in the army, but his brother was taken ill with sun stroke having spent so many hours on the river without any respite from the sun. Nurse Faye came to his rescue by confining him to his bed, and constantly sponging him down with cold water, until his temperature had returned to normal.

It was very rewarding to see the brothers had bonded as firmly as an Araldite fix thanks to their choice of holidays. The only news we caught up with years later was that Peter had been promoted to colonel of his regiment due to his professional dedication. Alas it contributed to the failure of his marriage.

OUR PAYING GUESTS

A couple of semi-retired folk once arrived unexpectedly in a camper van and parked in our courtyard. Were they going to camp out, instead of keeping their booking for half board and lodging? It soon transpired that the wife had only agreed to a long tour of the south of France provided they had a week's break at Le Mas Pradel, to enjoy some comfort and to catch up with their accumulation of dirty laundry, and of course to indulge themselves with Faye's home-cooked meals.

William, a summer guest

We soon discovered that Dr Bill and his wife were two of the most interesting guests we had that year. After the evening meal the three of us were invited to join them for coffee and conversation, which was a fine reward for toiling so hard throughout the summer heat to keep our business on track.

Bill and Joan recounted several of the experiences they had touring France, and many other European countries. Two of these highlighted the dangers of touring in their mobile home. The first event occurred in France when they had been unable to book a campsite for the night. Two gendarmes helpfully offered to lead them to a local site, so the tired and fed up couple, who had been searching for a place to sleep, were only too glad to follow the Good Samaritans. However, the site turned out to be nothing more than an enclosed area, with not a single van or tent in sight, and the bogus gendarmes were trying to close the gates and lock them inside. Bill realised that the uniforms were shoddy and incorrect, and they were about to be attacked if they remained trapped inside the enclosure. The engine was still running at the time so he jammed the gearbox in reverse and they shot out of the opening with the horn blaring, leaving the crooks with nothing more than eggs on their faces. As a result of this incident they devised a plan which they hoped would enable them to escape from any further attacks by bandits.

The following year they set off to tour Italy and were well rehearsed in their get-away plan. All went well and they managed to book campsites for each of the night's stops. Bill persuaded his wife Joan to drive to the viewpoint on a well-known volcano where the scenery was spectacular. The balmy night air and the beautiful panorama encouraged them to linger in the car park until it was dark. However, it was much too late to come down off the mountain and find the campsite they had booked, so they decided to spend the night in the empty car park and enjoy the sunrise.

An hour or so later the noise of feet shuffling on the gravel woke them with a start. Bill whispered, 'This is it, Joan. There are two men with iron bars outside, and I think they are going to use them.' Plan A was put into action. Joan dropped the lift-up roof, and Bill started the engine and kept his hand on the horn as they drove away, leaving the bandits empty-handed. Plan A certainly saved them both from being beaten up and robbed of their valuables. It is very sound advice to keep a suitable weapon tucked under the driver's seat, and to make sure that the camper van is always ready for a quick get-away.

Bill and Joan enjoyed their stay *chez nous* and by way of thank-you, invited us to stay in their service apartment which they kept for family and friends. Needless to say we enjoyed our break at the seaside and, of course, their company.

18

Law and Order

Back in the sixties I made friends with a clerk to a magistrate's court, who had been a superintendent in charge of my local police station. He told me that he dispensed justice for the youngsters who he caught stealing apples with a hearty whack on the backside with his rolled-up cape. The offenders were only too pleased with the punishment, because if they were reported to their parents, their father would give them a thorough thrashing with his belt and they'd get a tongue lashing as well from their mothers.

In the very first day on duty, when he was based in Bond Street police station, he was told to accompany his sergeant to the magistrate's court to see how justice worked. The first case was a regular, who had spent his night in the cells for being drunk and disorderly. The lady magistrate said, 'Before we proceed, sergeant, can you explain how the defendant came to have a black eye?' He replied that the policemen had great difficulty in getting the drunk up the steps at the back of the Black Maria, where he fell and this caused the injury. 'I quite understand,' the magistrate said, 'but how did the defendant get the other black eye?'

'Well m'lud he was just as violent when we tried to get him down the steps, and he tripped up and banged his head again.'

'As you know, sergeant, I do like to clear up any little misunderstandings before I deal with the case, and I find the defendant guilty as charged. He will be fined seven and sixpence.'

My friend confided in me that professional thieves who frequently evaded the arm of the law were often given the chance to plead guilty to a minor offence, and to ask for a number of other crimes to be taken into consideration. The professional crooks accepted it was just a hazard being caught, but it was a way of spending less time in prison. It was a popular ploy of the police, which cleared up lots of outstanding crimes.

These days justice has been hampered by the mountain of paperwork which the police are obliged to deal with, instead of showing their presence on the streets. Believe it or not, it is true that full-size cardboard cutouts of bobbies substitute for the real thing, who are coping with human rights, health and safety, bogus claims and greedy lawyers.

Common sense is unheard of these days and victims of crime are frequently punished when they defend themselves from louts and burglars.

Justice sometimes comes in unexpected ways, and I recall an amusing tale of a nightshift worker, who was sent home early. He returned home and quietly crept upstairs not wishing to disturb his wife's sleep. To his amazement a policeman's uniform was neatly laid on his bedside chair, and its owner was fast asleep beside his wife.

The thoughtful husband gathered up the uniform and returned it to the local police station without making any explanation as to where he had found it. He then returned home at his usual time, as though he had been working throughout the night. Justice did prevail. The randy copper was sacked for dereliction of duty, and the husband was delighted to have unshakeable grounds for his divorce.

The infamous case of the axe murderer was held up because the murder weapon couldn't be found and this lack of evidence was essential to get a guilty verdict. The police car which had conveyed the defendant to the police station was eventually cleaned and one of the staff found the axe underneath the rear seat. He promptly took it home to chop firewood. Justice prevailed by default, and the murder weapon can be seen in the Black Museum.

The French have a entirely different approach to law and order, and I hope my observations and opinions give an insight into the the French attitude towards crime and unsociable behaviour. In 1946 France was well nigh bankrupt and the gendarmes' pitiful incomes were supplemented by targeting the relative wealthy. Touring with my penfriend's family in Normandy we were caught in a cleverly arranged trap, set up by a gendarme motorcyclist and his accomplice.

LAW AND ORDER

The family's expensive car was a prime target, and the gendarme produced an official form and demanded a very substantial fine. I was told not to say anything because it would only make matters worse.

Red coupons were still in use for most commodities, especially for petrol after the war, and real hardship was commonplace, because there wasn't enough for everybody. Ration coupons were coloured red and these entitled everyone to the bare essentials. Pink coupons, on the other hand, could be purchased and these were acceptable everywhere. Needless to say it was the wealthy who fared well after the war, and the money raised to help supplement the state's income. I considered that this was a kind of state-run black market.

Being a curious teenager at the time I was fascinated to learn how the Normandy folk managed to keep alive, as there was little or no food anywhere, because the Germans had taken it all. My friend's family owned a engineering factory and happened to have a tin-making plant which they used to fill tins with coarse bread. I was honoured to taste the contents of their last remaining tin, which reminded me of a cube of cattle cake which I ate when I was eight years old. Their last great treasure was home-made liqueur made from wild flowers.

Most people in England closed their eyes to shopkeepers whose stock was kept under the counter, but they were only too glad have the chance of a special treat. However, the government managed to give enough rations to keep the population relatively well fed on a meagre but balanced diet, which was much healthier than today's diet which encourages obesity.

In France after a serious crime has been committed it is the Judge of Instruction who takes control of the proceedings, which are necessary to find the evidence which supports the case for a high court hearing. The general public put great importance in these judges, who go to great lengths in their quest to ascertain the facts, and they use a great deal of common sense in arriving at their conclusions.

It was of some interest to me when I read the daily paper to see what happened to the burglars, and crooks after the deliberation of the judge. One such case that I recall concerned a jeweller and his wife who were disturbed in their sleep above the shop by the sound of footsteps on the stairs. The husband grabbed his only weapon, which was a stout length of timber that he kept beneath the bed. He was just in time to see two burly men step into his bedroom, obviously intending to do the couple harm. However, the husband had decided that attack was the best defence, and he set about both of the burglars causing considerable injuries, which landed them both in hospital.

Needless to say the judge decided that the jeweller had no case to answer, as he was within his rights to defend himself, his wife and his goods. Numerous cases where the victims turned the tables on burglars and hold-up crooks always supported the victims.

A couple visited an expensive French furriers and selected a very expensive fur coat, paying for it with a cheque. The shop owner was completely satisfied that the couple were honest and wealthy enough to pay for the coat. However, the shop owner decided to telephone the bank to find if the purchaser had the funds to meet the cheque. Alas it was a dud, so he telephoned the police station and gave the details of the crooks' vehicle, and descriptions of his clients.

The police gave chase and no matter how hard they tried to stop the crooks, they continued to drive at breakneck speeds hoping to evade arrest. The policemen became alarmed at the danger the crooks were causing, and somehow they needed to stop the car before a serious accident occurred. Having exhausted every trick in the book, nothing deterred the crooks from escaping justice.

The two policemen decided that a warning shot from the observer's revolver might persuade the crooks that the police were determined to arrest them. The observer drew his pistol and fired the warning shot which passed through the passenger window, and the woman's neck. The vehicle did stop, but the woman died at the roadside.

The procedure for this case was to remove the policemen from their duties while the Judge of Instruction conducted his enquiries, which took several months. I believe that the observer who fired the fatal shot remained in the service. The driver of the get-away car was arrested and eventually he was sent to the High Court, where he was found guilty of numerous charges and sent to prison. After a long investigation the policeman who fired the fatal shot was exonerated on the grounds that the death was accidental.

Justice in France appears to err in favour of the police in this case and similar ones. The rights of the general public safeguard victims of crime.

I conclude that, in the UK, the rights of minorities take preference over those of law-abiding members of the general public. Our British newspapers and television abound with some of the most absurd cases, which anyone with a grain of common sense could see the futility of our bureaucracy and our courts to resolve cases by punishing criminals leniently and not helping the victims of crime.

I am however delighted to see at first hand that the police now carry straightforward instructions of exactly what they can do to offenders, at each stage of danger which they face. Extreme danger to a policeman during an arrest entitles them to use any means to safeguard their own lives, providing their actions can be justified. Helping our police goes a long way to create a safe society.

19

Local People and Local History

Our neighbours

Daniel and Lillian lived in the converted farm building at the end of our driveway. They became our firm friends, and whenever we needed advice or help they didn't hesitate for a moment to help us. I remember the first time we had an impromptu lunchtime party in the forecourt, and we started to play boules in the driveway, before tucking in to the food which Faye had laid out on tables in the shade of the acacia trees. In next to no time Daniel and Lillian had joined us bearing their contribution towards the meal. Jean Pierre and Sylvette had taken the trouble of disturbing the local baker from his Sunday afternoon siesta, to open his shop and sell them a superb gateau, so they could contribute too. The party was a great success and the English proved that they could play boules as well as the French neighbours.

The only problem we had during our eleven years in the Mas was an old car which belonged to Jean Pierre. It remained dumped next to our car park and was an eyesore. Not wishing to upset Jean Pierre and his family, we asked his nephew Daniel how we could get the car removed without causing an offence to our immediate neighbours. Within a week the eyesore had been towed away, and the matter was never mentioned.

The locals accepted us as soon as we had officially started paying rates, and had settled into our Mas. Later on we received our *cartes de séjour*, and started paying land taxes. Exchanging my driving licence was straightforward, but joining the national health system proved to be very bureaucratic. Finally we had completed all the necessary procedures to become residents in France.

The downside was that everybody expected us to speak French. However, as long as we made an effort the locals always encouraged us, and even gesticulations substituted for our lack of correct grammar or vocabulary. We always appreciated the way we were made to feel at home in our adopted country, as we were one day when we visited a rose growers' festival high up in the Cevenne mountains. The venue was a large field where the tables and seats were arranged round the shaded perimeter of the field and a large marquee served as a cafeteria. We all felt ill at ease because we had not paid an entrance fee, and we were both hungry and thirsty.

We need not have worried because several of the members realised that we were strangers, and they invited us to join them at an adjacent table, and then advised us to queue up in the cafeteria for free meals. This generous hospitality reflected the natural kindness we were to find from the folk in our region.

A little bit of history

During the early days of our occupation of the Mas, we tried to obtain records and maps from the Departmental Archives, which was responsible for recording historical sites of interest. The answers to our enquiries were very disappointing. 'There are such an enormous number of these sites it is impossible to catalogue them all.'

A good example is the remains of a Roman Villa close to Les Volets Rouge, where we spent five weeks searching for our future home. It is situated high up in the hills, and it was most probably used by a Roman dignitary, as a retreat from the unbearable heat of the summers. Our friend Lisa showed us the remains of the building, which consisted of the ground floor and the central heating system which was still intact. Her children loved searching for and finding artefacts. This unprotected site is known by very few of the locals, and its location is very difficult to find, so it remains unrecorded.

The very first record of a written language was carved on an outcrop of rock, somewhere in the Alpes-Maritimes. The most interesting site in Saint Ambroix is 'Les Dugas' which is a rocky outcrop some hundred feet or so high, and situated right in the heart of the town.

LOCAL PEOPLE AND LOCAL HISTORY

Roman Triumphal Arch (circa pre 1000 AD), Pont d'Arc

Another arch!

Sacrificial murders were carried out on a smooth flat rock which resembled an altar. It has a bowl-shaped hole carved in it where the blood was collected. Beside the altar is a cave where the high priests carried out the ceremonies before they threw the bodies out of an opening in the cave, onto the ground below. Slight traces of the blood remain in the hole on the altar to this day.

The religious wars between the Catholics and the Protestants had a profound impact on the way French society evolved, and even today the two religious groups tend to go their own way. The pharmacists and other professional bodies tend to be known by their religious sects. The three of us happened to choose the Protestant pharmacy because the other one was not friendly towards unbelievers.

Back in the days when Protestants were persecuted if they did not renounce their religion, punishments varied, but the preachers were murdered in the most revolting way, usually in public places, as an example of what might happen to the followers. Close to our Mas the preachers held services in a very secluded spot, where watchers kept a look-out for the soldiers who lived in the town with the local folk. It was their job to root out the heretics.

We discovered an amazing priest hole which was big enough for a preacher to hide until it was safe to get away. The hole was lined with straw for bedding and the ventilation was provided by gaps in the pointing of the outer wall, and one of the floor tiles in the salon covered a small hole through which the food and water could be lowered to the man hiding below. A very small cross was carved on one of the two front doors, as a secret sign to show that the house was a religious one, and sanctuary would be given to anyone in need of hiding from the soldiers. The discovery of a fossilised bone of a saint was recognition of the good work done on behalf of the Protestant sect. It was also to ensure that good luck would remain in the house provided it stayed there. Bonne Chance seemed to be an appropriate name for this book, because the three of us certainly spent eleven happy years in our home.

The name Mas was given to the principal dwellings in the south of France, which had evolved gradually as each new generation built their own accommodation connected to the original house by a keystone or a bulk of timber which the parents put in place to show

LOCAL PEOPLE AND LOCAL HISTORY

Le Mas Pradel

A bird's-eye view

Autumn 1992

where the next extension was to be. Gradually these Mas grew into small hamlets or villages. Our own Mas was extended by two stages only, because the workers on the estate lived in a small hamlet a short distance further up the hill, called Perrières. When we bought the property we needed to know its address, but the only name used by the locals was Le Mas. We inadvertently named it Le Mas Pradel after the name of a previous owner, but in reality it should have taken the name Le Mas Perrières. The ancient, relatively small building became large enough to have part of it given over to the production of silk. It was also fortified with firing ports on the second floor level, and some of these were used to ventilate the silk worms, but the most recent of these was found hidden behind the plasterwork in a bedroom on the second floor. The pigeon loft was a sign of opulence because it provided fresh meat during the winter months.

20

Mind Your Language

Summer 1947. My French pen pal and I, together with his extended family, were touring in northern France in two cars. Our objective one night was to reach the city of Rennes during the annual festival, but it was midnight before Michel's father had bribed the manager of a frightfully expensive hotel to squeeze eight of us in the last available rooms. He also had to pay the overworked kitchen staff an obscene bonus for them to provide us with the finest meal I could ever remember eating. It was almost 2 am before we had consumed several lobsters, and the other three courses. Michel asked me, tongue in cheek, if I had eaten enough, to which I replied, '*Je suis a pleine*', which was my interpretation of 'I am full up'.

Michel burst out laughing at my faux pas, so I asked him not to let on to the others what I had said. Nevertheless the family and some of the staff were very curious about what I had said. Michel and I shared a room so I was able to make him promise not to embarrass me any more. I fell asleep assured that I would have heard the last of my faux pas.

In the morning Michel made an excuse for me to go ahead of him to the dining room for breakfast. I opened our door and found a crowd of guests all heading towards the lift and without exception they all seemed to be laughing. One of them asked how many kittens I was expecting; another asked me how far gone was my pregnancy.

I was mortified, but the worst was yet to come. The bell hop signalled me to step into the lift, and he then closed the door leaving the crowd behind. Much to my annoyance he sniggered as he stopped the lift and opened the door to reveal a huge dining room packed with guests who gave me a round of applause for my faux pas which had given them all the best laugh they had at my expense.

Autumn 1984. We were beginning to get to know our immediate neighbours, and all three of us hoped we had made a good impression on Daniel and Lillian, so it was natural for me to be pleased that Lillian was interested in my son Paul whom she had already met. 'What does your son do for his living?' she asked. I replied in French that he was a very well-known *voilier*. Unfortunately my pronunciation sounded like *voler*. Instead of me telling her that Paul was a well-known sailor, I had said that he was a well-known thief and a cheat. This did not go down very well at the time, especially as Daniel was the chief of the municipal police, but I managed to save Paul's good name and reputation.

The French are very tolerant of newcomers who make a hash of trying to speak their language. The important thing to remember is that they will respect you if you make an attempt at using even just a few basic words.

Once a month the committee of the English Circle met to plan the following month's activities, and as usual it was difficult to find club members to undertake the organisation of the activity they had suggested. An attractive young French woman had recently joined our circle of English-speaking friends, in order to brush up her English in preparation for her degree. She was coping very well with our debate, although by nature she was very reticent about voicing her own opinions.

She suddenly plucked up courage and said, 'I have a good idea for our next activity.' This caught everyone's attention. She then said, 'I think we should all bring a musical instrument, and then we can all play with ourselves.'

All the English members found it almost impossible to refrain from laughing out loud.

The French wife of Faye's friend recounted her most embarrassing moment when she was married to an English soldier. The poor woman had no English whatsoever, and she was left alone when she first came to London because her husband was posted abroad.

Like most women she had a passion for shoes, and one day she plucked up courage to ask the owner of the local shoe shop if he had any sealskin slippers for sale. Unfortunately her English failed her and she used the French word for seal instead. The outraged shopkeeper refused to serve her, but she repeated her request for the slippers without any luck. When she was about to repeat her request the shopkeeper physically ejected her from the shop. '*Phoque* skin slippers' sounded like condoms to the shopkeeper!

At the beginning of our first November in the Mas, we were very impressed with all the wonderful chrysanthemums that were on sale all over our town. We decided to decorate the entrance to our courtyard with the most delightful blooms we had ever seen. Somewhere along the track we had gone off the rails, because our neighbours had behaved in a very strange way towards our flower arrangements, and they lowered their eyes each time they saw us.

It was dear Lillian, who lived at the end of our road in the old farm building, who finally braced herself to ask who had died in our family. It was a few days later when we realised that All Saints Day is celebrated by placing chrysanthemums on the tombs and graves of the deceased. We joined the long procession of mourners, and various military representatives, local dignitaries, and of course Lillian's husband who represented the municipal police.

Late one Saturday evening we heard our neighbour's car drive past the Mas, and we wondered if our Chief of Police had been called out on business. If that was the case it was unusual because Saint Ambroix was a very law-abiding town. The following morning I drove down to the newsagents for *The Times*, and on the way up our long driveway I was surprised to see a motorcycle leaning against our ancient bridge. For the life of me I could not think who on earth would dump a perfectly good motorcycle. I decided to give Daniel a telephone call in case he might know who owned it.

Daniel was grateful for the call and he went on to explain how it came to be propping up the wall of the bridge. He had been called out to help the gendarmes find a thief who had made off with a substantial haul from a break-in. He had gone to ground somewhere in our town. Daniel was an expert on tracking wild boar because he kept a local hunt's pack of large hunting dogs, so he put his expertise to good use.

Unfortunately he finally lost his quarry after spending the best part of the night without any sleep. My telephone call prompted Daniel to see if his own motorcycle was still safely locked inside his garage. Apparently the thief had broken into the garage and had been hiding there until the hunt had been given up. Then he pushed the motorcycle as far as the bridge and abandoned it because it was out of fuel. I can imagine how embarrassing it would have been if Daniel's colleagues and the gendarmes ever found out that the thief had spent most of the night safely holed-up in Daniel's garage.

One of our favourite venues for a good party was Ted and Joan's house, which was a beautifully restored village property that boasted a good size swimming pool. We could be sure of a jolly good time whenever we were invited to one of their generous parties. It happened that Ted had invited the three of us, and one of the Dambuster pilots and his wife, who had been a BBC Producer, to accompany us to his party.

All went well, and we anticipated having a good time with our hospitable hosts. Ted welcomed us when we arrived, but Joan seemed to be in a bad mood for some reason, and there was a definite chill in the atmosphere. Ted was already drunk and ignored his wife's remonstrations about his drinking, and he started playing German oompah music as loudly as possible. By this time you could cut the atmosphere with a knife, so we agreed to take the Ivesons back to our own home for the rest of the evening, and make do with what we could find in the fridge to keep our hunger at bay.

The makeshift evening was a great success considering the circumstances. Ted apologised the next day when he had sobered up and explained what had occurred the afternoon before. The house next door had been restored, and when Joan returned from her architectural business she found that the roof over part of the property had been damaged by wet cement, and this had destroyed the beautiful effect of the Spanish tiled roof. Joan was an architect of some repute and she 'went ballistic' to see that the presentation of her home had been degraded by the carelessness of the builders. Naturally she demanded in no uncertain manner that the builders clean the roof immediately, and to placate her wrath they set to work with a high water-pressure machine which removed the offending cement.

Joan could not bear looking at the men on the roof so she went shopping, but when she returned home she found that her studio had been flooded by the deluge of pressurised water which had destroyed many of her architectural plans and sketches. Only an architect could comprehend the enormity of the anguish Joan must have suffered when she saw what had happened to decades of her creative work.

Sometimes when I start a conversation in French and misuse the exact word needed to start the dialogue, it can be embarrassing or amusing. I wanted to ask Lillian our neighbour for some information about the planning regulations as I was hoping to build an extension to our cottage to house a bathroom. However, she was away shopping so I tried to ask her daughter about my problem. Unfortunately I used another less popular word which got me off to a confused start, so I said that I would phone her mother later on. Lillian phoned when she came home and spoke to Faye, and said that she could not understand why I wanted some jam.

I managed to explain to Lillian what I wanted to know about the planning regulations, and I was pleasantly surprised to hear her response. As long as you keep on good terms with your neighbours, no one will report you, and in any case Daniel has the post of planning inspector, in addition to his job as the chief of the municipal police. Needless to say the extension went ahead without any problems.

Before we took possession of the Mas, Alan wrote to the mayor and asked what regulations might effect the renovations, and the installation of a septic tank sewerage system. The reply was very straight forward: Any alterations to the façade of the house must be applied for, and the only requirement for the sewerage system is that it works.

What a breath of fresh air and common sense applies to the renovation of the old properties in France. It has encouraged many foreigners like ourselves to upgrade the towns and country.

21

Filming with Mai

One thing our friend Mai Zetterling and I had in common was experience of mean people. She recounted one of her experiences with a seriously wealthy man, who had proposed financing a film based on a story he fancied. Mai was also taken with the idea, so she arranged to meet the financier in a restaurant situated close to a well-known bookshop, where she was sure that he could find a copy of the chosen story.

The financier arrived minus the essential book, so Mai asked him why he had not brought it with him. His reply astounded Mai, because he said he could not find a single copy of the story as there was only a trilogy available, and he was not prepared to spend the extra money on it. Mai left the man wondering why she had walked away from him.

My own modest experience was a friend of ours who had offered to wash up after the evening meals in return for bed and breakfast. However, he arrived with his mistress and expected us to provide them with a double bedroom, breakfast and evening meals. During their stay they latched onto some of our well-to-do friends, and one them invited the three of us and them to a party. Faye reminded them that it was the custom to take at least a good bottle of wine. Their chosen tipple was an eighty pence bottle of beer.

At the end of their stay we were obliged to ask our scrounging friends to pay for their telephone calls which had been substantial. At first he declined to settle his debt, but instead threw a wobbly before shaking the moths from his purse.

Mai herself was very generous to her friends when she was in funds, and they sometimes took advantage of her. However, the three of us were her adopted family so when she was hard up we repaid her kindness. Whatever was going on in her life, Mai always included us no matter how important her guests might be. One day she confided in us that she was anxious about a part she was hoping to get, and when she said that it was a lead part as one of the witches in a film of that name, Alan told her that she was made for the part.

During Mai's absence from the Mazel Faye took all of her calls including those from well-known Hollywood personalities. By way of a thank you for Faye's friendship and professional help, the three of us received an invitation to attend a film shoot of *Robin Hood*, which was to take place in the gorge of the Tarn.

Alan declined the invitation because the temperature in the gorge was going to be close on freezing. Faye and I set off not knowing how we would be received when we arrived on set.

The journey to our destination was one the three of us had already made during the summer. We had discovered how the ancient inhabitants had constructed their homes without the use of timber, because there were hardly any trees in and around the gorge of the Tarn. We also visited one of the early hamlets which was cleverly disguised amongst the rocky landscape, to deter the roaming bandits who might want to pillage and rape. It was intriguing to imagine where Mai had chosen the precise setting for her part of the Robin Hood film, as the gorge and the surrounding landscape seemed a million miles away from Sherwood Forest, where trees are in abundance.

We were awoken from these thoughts by a motorcycle gendarme who instructed us to halt, and demanded to know where we were going. I told him that Faye and I were invitees of Mai Zetterling, and we were bound for a local chateau where the company was based. He dropped his officious stance, and said that we would have to wait for a while, as the road was closed to prevent any traffic noise from spoiling the take.

Our arrival at the chateau was premature, because the crew would be late for the midday meal which was to be served in the hospitality marquee, and we were invited to wait there for the crowd to arrive.

Much to our delight Mai made straight away to join us, and as the more important members took their seats we were introduced to some scruffy-looking characters, dressed in little more than sackcloth and not washed for weeks. Strange though it may be, Faye recognised two of the actors. One of these had stayed in Faye and Alan's guest house in Plymouth, where their son worked in the Hoe Theatre and members of the cast often joined guests while they were on tour.

Our lunch hour spent in the company of witty and pleasant people passed all too quickly. I felt flattered that our friend Mai made it obvious that she was proud to have our company. The best was yet to come when we scrambled down the makeshift path, which had been made so that the scene could be filmed in virgin woodland overlooking the river. It had been perfectly planned because the mist caused by the near zero temperature, and the midday sun, gave a striking atmosphere as the actors approached the camera.

The take was nearly ruined when the mounted camera on its railway lines almost shot off into space towards the river, when a piece of gear gave way. The cast found it difficult trying to act their parts, when parts of them felt as though they would drop off in the freezing atmosphere. Nevertheless, the cast got on with the shoot with some prompting from Mai. I found it strange to see the real people at their lunch and then watch them take on their new identities.

Faye was finding that the near-freezing temperature was making her colour turn to blue instead of her usual deep tan, and she was very surprised when Mai stopped filming and walked across to ask her if she needed some extra clothing. We decided that it would be more prudent if we retired to our car and made our way home.

In retrospect we enjoyed our glimpse into Mai's professional life and the way we had been treated by such an internationally acclaimed actress, writer, producer, and instigator of the new-look TV advertising. Throughout our friendship with Mai we met many of her friends and business acquaintances. She also spoke about some of her well-known friends which I found to be very illuminating, but too confidential for me to put in print.

22

The Festival Season

France celebrates the release of the prisoners from the notorious prison in Paris called Le Bastille, because it was the tipping point in the birth of the first Republic of France. Thus 14 July has been celebrated throughout the country and its overseas French protectorates every year.

The Cultural Minister has the responsibility for ensuring that every commune has its fair share of the finance, so that everyone in the entire country can enjoy themselves. Holidaymakers who are fortunate

Festival time

Saint Ambroix

to be in France from 14 July onwards can easily visit different festivals every day of their stay without travelling very far.

Our first invitation to one of these festivals was a very simple affair and it was out of season, although it was in season for the mayor of a small local village called Les Marges to choose a chestnut and local wine tasting event. Many of the local inhabitants had originally fled the Civil War in Spain, and they certainly made us welcome to their 'barbecue style' evening. Two of the locals offered to give us a hand with our renovations of our Mas. One of these kind folk called José gave me some invaluable practical advice on laying floor tiles. In fact he demonstrated how to do this by laying all the floor tiles in our new dining room, after the three of us had dug up the old floor which flooded each time it rained, laid a drainage system, and made the concrete waterproofed floor.

The following Saturday José and Angel arrived unexpectedly, with a rabbit, a barbecue stove and some local wine, and then prepared and cooked our midday meal. Afterwards we all retired to the first floor terrace where Faye persuaded the lads to demonstrate Spanish

THE FESTIVAL SEASON

tap dancing. Our lunch break continued into the late evening, accompanied by home-brewed music, dancing and laughter. Our revelry helped us to forget the hard physical work we had been doing, and the prospect of the several more years of real hard labour before the restorations would be finished.

The following morning I collected our *Times* from the newsagent as usual, His greeting was not the customary '*Bonjour Monsieur*,' but, 'I wish you had invited my wife and me to your party.' His house, I might add, was a good quarter of a kilometre from our own.

We saw the other end of the festival spectrum during our holiday in Nice. The procession was incredibly long with its multitude of floats, and bands from every part of the region. The onlookers were all in great form and made friends with the nearest folk who were squeezed together like sardines in a tin.

Alan started clapping the police band which preceded a large float adorned with the most delectable topless young women that any red blooded males would fancy. One such male who was standing next to Alan, Faye and our two Cornish guests and me, waved his finger

Alan, Faye, Richard; Besseges market

in rebuke and said, 'We never cheer the Police in France, only the half naked girls.'

The large towns and cities spend a fortune on these festivals, and there is a lot of rivalry in providing the best and most popular event in the region. However, my own preference is for the smaller events like the Saint Ambroix festival. Some of the smaller events attract some world-class professional musicians and groups.

The population of Saint Ambroix is about four thousand, but in the season it increases threefold, and the festivities extend for six days. Tables and chairs stretch from one end of the main street to the other, and these provide some comfort for those who spend their time dancing in one of the town squares, where *musique de papa* is provided for the parents and grandparents, who love the old time dancing, and need some refreshment. The younger generations live it up dancing to modern music in another part of town. One year we listened to three bands playing simultaneously in town, and we could hear the music clearly from our first floor terrace, which was more than a half a kilometre away from the revellers.

A happy face

THE FESTIVAL SEASON

The following afternoon the three of us and our guests watched as the floats and bands passed by. Daniel our chief of police led the procession, until he reached where we stood. Much to our surprise he stopped the procession, walked across to us, and shook our hands. He then resumed his post at the head of the procession.

Mai, her best Swedish girlfriend and the daughter met up with our crowd at the town market place where a group was playing *musique de papa*. The dense crowd was in party spirit and Mai and her well-known actress friend joined in the fun. I suddenly discovered that I was dancing with a delectable young Swedish starlet. Meanwhile someone in the crowd recognised Mai and asked Faye if it was her. However, Mai wanted to keep her anonymity so she nudged Faye and said, 'Tell her I am Mrs Brown.'

One of the most remarkable things about the festivals and other events where so many people gather is the lack of a police presence. This is due to the natural good behaviour of the parents, and the high expectations they have that their offspring will not disgrace themselves. I know from my own experience that to be seen drunk and out of control in public is never condoned.

Most English parents would say 'Pigs might fly' if someone said that their teenagers only drank in moderation. However, in Saint Ambroix it's not the pigs that fly, but a full-sized bull, inflated and released from a tower on top of a steep hill at the entrance to the town. This celebrates an event in the town's history when a real bull was thrown from the same spot and its carcase roasted to feed the town's folk. These inflated bulls are carried away on the wind, and I wondered what passengers in passing aircraft would say if they saw a bull flying alongside them.

23

Winter Weather

Our private road retaining wall collapsed, and it caused something of a crisis, as our two neighbouring properties and our own had no access other than on foot. Daniel our policeman organised everything needed to rebuild the retaining wall, including the manpower. The middle of the winter is hardly the best time to start a major project, especially as it had started to snow. However, Daniel assured me that there would not be a problem as snow was a rarity at this time of the year. Within less than an hour we were all stripped down to t-shirts, and sweating profusely, as the snow fell. The job was completed within three days thanks to our neighbours' help.

Another example of unexpected snow was when our roof was being restored in the middle of our first winter, when the builder booked a late January date for the commencement of the work. The lads removed the entire roof over the family bedroom, and left it uncovered when they stopped work for the day. The boss was quite unconcerned that the room was uncovered as he assured us that there was no chance of snow or rain during the night.

Just after midnight Faye woke up to find that snow was falling so hard that it would damage the building. An unexpected telephone call rallied the builders who covered the open room, and all was well.

The two photographs which I have included give some idea of the contrasts in the winter weather. The skies are generally an incredible deep blue, and the wisps of high-altitude clouds are brilliant ice white. The air is so clear of toxic waste it is possible to see details of the moon which townies have never seen. Surprisingly the locals remain housebound whenever it snows, missing the fun which youngsters enjoy back in the UK. The day before the photo of our long driveway

Midwinter blue sky

A rare sight

was taken, Saint Ambroix was covered with some six inches of snow. Alan, Faye and I decided to walk into town and pop in to our local bar for a coffee, but the only sign of life in town was a solitary snowman. The only footprints in the main road were our own, and a set of ski tracks confirmed that there was a least one other living soul in town.

Emboldened by our foray into town we decided to visit the viewpoint on our nearest proper mountain. The last section of the journey was on a very tortuous small road which climbed to a height of some four thousand feet. Faye, her sister-in-law, Brian her son, and I were rewarded by a fantastic panorama in crystal clear visibility. Mont Blanc was on the left, on the border of Switzerland and France. The Mediterranean with its deep blue colour, and the curvature of the earth was straight ahead, and finally the mountains which form the border between Spain and France.

Our journey was well worthwhile and Brian and his aunt Judy had a brief snowball fight before we packed our bags and set off on a very long downhill track in deep snow. I was already feeling that I had made a serious mistake in undertaking our outing, as we had not seen any other vehicles on the mountain 'white grade roads' which are single track and difficult. We had barely got under way when the snow started to fall, and within less than a quarter of an hour a blizzard closed in around us.

Faye and I had once travelled from Benfleet in Essex to Plymouth in the worst snow storm for many years. We travelled on the M4 on the only lane open, but the windscreen of my small sports car froze up and I navigated by watching the central crash barrier through the side screen, and stopping each time I saw a red glow through the frozen windscreen.

At one stage I was so desperate to urinate I stopped underneath a flyover, and relieved myself whilst the snow fell so thick it was black. I believe our sports car was the only vehicle to complete the journey from London to Exeter that night, and we were complimented by the police who helped us get back on the road at one stage.

Having driven through London, which was cluttered with abandoned taxis, buses and cars, and spent the night in the Exeter Services because the roads were all closed, before we moved the cones and successfully reached our destination at Plymouth, I was surprised just how dangerous the mountain roads in France can be if you get caught out in a blizzard.

After such a nailbiting visit to Mont Loziere in the middle of winter, the locals would not have been impressed by my foolhardy choice of venues. My one saving grace was the fact that the road had not been used, so the virgin snow provided some grip for the tyres. The other factor was the return journey was downhill all the way so we were able to keep some momentum all the way home The visibility was so poor at times it was difficult to make out where the road edges ended.

Arriving home to a log fire in the dining room, and the kitchen range at full blast, made me realise what a wonderful home we had. The welcome from our two dogs and Alan's cups of tea was just the icing on the cake.

Our first winter lasted for only ten days, and nine of our remaining winters, with the exception of the one I have mentioned, were very mild. The dark blue skies constantly kept our spirits high.

24

A Walk in the Garrigue

Joan was one of our good friends from Cornwall who loved our lifestyle, and always paid her way when staying with us, in spite of having a very small income. Our relatively wealthy friends tended to expect us to keep them on our small pensions, so we appreciated her company even more. We particularly enjoyed showing Joan our beautiful scenery, as it gave Jasper and Katie the chance to run free and nose around for interesting trophies to take home. Katie would make for the nearest pond and wallow in the none too clean water where she was in her element.

Our favourite local walk was on a track which wound its way through the garrigue (scrubland), and during the late summer evenings the heady aroma of wild herbs was intoxicating. The panorama as we walked northwards stretched our eyes to the distant mountains which were silhouetted against the dusty-coloured backdrop of the approaching night sky. During our previous visit to our dog-walking spot I noticed several stone beehive-shaped buildings, so I made up my mind to investigate them on my own, because the stony undergrowth looked to be full of pitfalls, and large rocks.

Alan, Faye, Joan and I set off with our two excited dogs early in the afternoon, and I suggested that everyone except myself should go ahead on the regular circuit, while I visited the strange buildings. However, Faye and Joan refused to miss out on my archaeological departure in spite of my warnings. Joan took Faye's walking stick and the reckless pair set off after me.

Disaster suddenly struck poor Faye, who was gracefully leaping from one flat rock to another when she landed on a large rock which gave way and catapulted her onto the rocks several feet below. Blood streamed from her face and mouth, and for a ghastly moment I thought she might die. Alan said that he was unable to help lift Faye, and Joan was too elderly and frail to help me carry her over such dangerous terrain towards our parked car many hundreds of yards away.

I estimated that Faye would be in the greatest danger if I left her in the care of Joan and Alan while I fetched the emergency services, because of the time it would take to get her to the Accident and Emergency Department at Alès General Hospital. The wisest solution in my opinion was to get her on her feet, and with Joan and me supporting her we could make our way very carefully to the car. Once we made it back to the track I ran like hell to the car, and in no time at all I had collected our party and drove at high speed directly to Dr Gougas's surgery.

Our good friend and doctor gave Faye a thorough check-up and then told me to recline her seat fully and drive post haste to the hospital. We arrived at the A&E Department to find that the staff were planning to start their weekend as soon as possible, and they showed little interest in dealing with an inconvenient patient. Faye had a compound fracture of her wrist but no one was available to set it. The excuse for the lack of treatment was that there was no need for any surgical intervention. My protest about the lack of treatment finally produced a single painkiller, and a triangular bandage to support the arm. Faye was told that it would be three days before her fracture could be reset. We decided to seek help in one of the private clinics, but even there Faye had to wait until the staff had finished their weekend before the fracture was finally set.

The extent of her injuries was severe; a suspected fracture of her upper jaw with the loss of almost all of her top teeth. The arm and wrist were reset but she was warned that she might lose her hand because of the severity of the damage.

The president of our English Circle was enraged at the treatment of his vice president, who had assisted the hospital by being on morgue duty when ten schoolchildren had died in a coach crash. He was in the process of making a formal complaint about the treatment Faye had received when she declined to support his complaint, rather than get the staff into trouble.

25

Montpellier Airport

Pick-ups and drop-offs at the airport were a frequent job I had during the summer, when members of our extended family, friends, and some paying guests did not wish to hire a car at the airport. My very first drop-off was particularly important for one of our guests who was over anxious to be on time. I had allowed enough time for the journey, but Alan insisted that there was plenty of time for him to pop into an antique shop which we were passing en route to the airport. I found it almost impossible to prise him away from his beloved antiques, which left me with barely enough time to make the flight. I kept my foot hard down on the accelerator all the way and my eyes were aching from watching out for the police speed traps. However, our guest managed to get his foot in the door of the departure lounge as it was closing.

Subsequent visits to the airport were far more relaxed, and we found that the family-sized concourse was friendly, unlike the huge ones in the major airports. We even found time to pop down the road and enjoy a swim in the Med which made the journey so worthwhile, especially when our guests joined us on the beach.

On one occasion Faye and I were surprised to meet Mai waiting for her friend in the reception area, so we enjoyed a chat and a coffee before we departed. Afterwards we were about to drive away when Mai stopped us to ask where she had to pay for the parking. Faye gave me a nudge in the ribs and said, 'For goodness sake, you had better take Mai back into the concourse and show her where the machine is.'

It just happened that a jumbo jet was due to take off soon and lots of passengers were hurrying towards the main entrance. Mai

Faye contemplating taking a dip or canoeing

promptly put her arm round my waist and started recounting in a stage whisper what she anticipated doing on our fictitious dirty weekend. Those passengers who were close enough to overhear what Mai suggested, continued on their way with the most startled expressions on their faces, which would have been worthy of inclusion in one of Mai's films.

Another visit to the airport was to collect Mai after she had been filming. Faye and I were surprised that the customs staff kept her waiting until all the passengers had been processed. She finally appeared carrying a decorated barge brush which she started to use, then asking the passengers if they would kindly move as she had to clean the floor. A naval officer called her bluff by saying that he knew she was Mai Zetterling.

Her timing for taking centre stage was perfect, and at parties she would hang back until she had everyone's attention before proceeding with her joke or one of her stories. She was very good at 'one liners', like the time she had broken her arm and the surgeon needed to remove her bra, which he managed without taking her pullover off, as if by magic. 'I see you are very experienced,' she said. The surgeon laughed and told her that he had recognised her.

For some time Alan had found the airport run rather tiring in the hot weather, and he decided not to accompany Faye and me when we were due to collect our friend Joan for a two-week holiday. Alan suggested that Faye should visit one of his close friends, Gerald Durrell, who lived in the Chateau Sommiere. He was anxious to learn how his pal had settled down in our part of France, and how the rest of his family were faring. Faye decided to call on Gerald on our way back home. Joan and I would keep a low profile as we had no connection with the well-known author. We found the chateau without any difficulty, but the gate had no means of opening it, so Faye waited for some time before Gerald opened his front door and demanded to know who he was talking to. Faye mentioned that she was married to Alan Greene, whereupon she was escorted inside his home, leaving Joan and me to fritter our time away as we contemplated what was going on inside.

Eventually Faye appeared looking rather the worse for drinking one of Gerald's vintage wines. It transpired that Faye was asked where she would like to be entertained, either in the kitchen or in his bedroom. He said that most of the ladies who wanted something from him either wanted his autograph or a baby! He asked Faye if Alan had visited his half-cousin Graham Greene, who lived in Antibes not far from Nice. She replied that Alan was never one to bother his wealthy relations. Gerald said that there was going to be a party in the near future, that Mai was on the list of guests, and that the Mas Pradel folk would be invited. Alan firmly refused to visit either Gerald or Graham. Alan never pulled rank on anybody, and many of his friends never knew that he had been a captain in the Royal Engineers, and had been offered rank of colonel if he had remained in the army after the war. He had been captured by the Japs and tortured, before being rescued by the Ghurkas.

26

More Friends

Augustine (Gus) and Lisa

During our stay in Les Volets Rouge, the owner introduced us to a Dutchman and his Kentish wife who lived with their three children high up in the nearby hills. Circumstances were to lead us to become enduring friends with this hippy family.

Gus, his mother, brother and sister spent their lives during the Second World War hiding from the Germans, living in the forest and woodlands, living off the land in makeshift shelters. It was to be the beginning of Gus's love of nature, and his desire to become a farmer when he grew up. However, his natural flair for languages gave him another career, which incarcerated him in a university teaching Russian.

A camping holiday romance started when Gus pinned flowers to Lisa's tent! At the end of her holiday she could not bear to be parted from her new love, so she decided to accept the offer of living on Gus's boat, providing that she found work, which was by no means easy as she did not speak a word of Dutch. Nevertheless her strong personality helped her make friends and learn the language, and she worked very hard for her living.

One Monday morning Gus was luxuriating in his bath, while he contemplated his future if he was to continue with his detached urban way of life. The prospects of years of teaching, and being reprimanded by a council officer because he was in the habit of leaving his lawn unmown was dismal. He could not tolerate the way the state controlled everyone. He decided that he would persuade Lisa to marry him and they would sell up and search for a smallholding, somewhere in the south of France where the climate was ideal for the purpose they had in mind.

They eventually found a semi-derelict Mas whose owner let them camp out in it on a temporary basis. This gave them the opportunity to search for a suitable and cheap smallholding somewhere near Saint Ambroix, which had a very good climate. Little did we know that one day we would buy their makeshift home. A further coincidence found them renting Les Volets Rouge on a short lease while they waited to move into their chosen paradise, which consisted of two habitable buildings that needed a lot of major work done on them. A delightful paddock and a considerable spread of woodland was all that they had hoped to find, and at a modest price.

During their long wait for possession Gus devoted his time to translating as his means of income, but with three children and a wife to maintain, the family was obliged to tighten their belts. Having taken possession of the property, the one thing that the family enjoyed was the total freedom to roam their large woodland, and to have the time and opportunity to commune with nature.

From time to time we climbed the steep stone-flagged path which was part of an ancient system of pathways the farmers used to move their animals from one place to another to avoid being seen by bandits and the King's soldiers, because these tracks were so well hidden by the forests.

In spite of the family's lack of money they always made us very welcome, by giving us some of their home-grown produce. We always looked forward to our visits at their fascinating home, and in return Gus often called at Le Mas Pradel when he was in our vicinity, where he charmed our guests and friends.

Gus introduced an ancient breed of pigs which he reared and then sold the meat to restaurants that specialised in Cevennolle food. Unfortunately the reality of maintaining their lifestyle and feeding the children proved to be exceedingly harder than the rose-tinted expectations they had in their days in Holland. I remember that they were feeding the children with pumpkin which turned their skins bright orange, because it was the only crop they had to live on for some weeks.

We were so surprised once when Gus arrived bearing a very large gateau as a gift, so we assumed he was in funds for a change. One of our friends warned us that he collected waste food from a bakery, which he fed to his pigs, and he kept the best items for his family.

One day Gus returned with an old bath which he said was to be installed in their home. Lisa was delighted at the prospect of bathing indoors after so many years. However, her delight soon turned sour when Gus told her that he was going to use it for washing his pigs before they were slaughtered, and then he said she could clean it and use it herself. This was the tipping point in their marriage, which had deprived Lisa of the basic conveniences any housewife would expect.

Several years later she had moved into Gus's brother's chateau-like property which even boasted a turret, and extensive land. Their relationship lasted until her partner decided he wanted a housewife dedicated to looking after his every need. His solution was to buy a young Asian wife who came with her entire family, who were only too glad to reside in their own accommodation.

Gus's brother was a well-known Dutch author who specialised in the paranormal, and produced scripts for Dutch TV. He was the complete opposite to his brother, very suave, attractive and his English was well nigh perfect, but he could not bring himself to stay in the primitive conditions on Gus's pig farm.

One of Gus's regular visits to Le Mas Pradel coincided with a telephone call which informed me that my youngest daughter had been admitted to a hospital somewhere in Germany, and that it was unlikely that my ex wife would let me know exactly where to find her, or what she was doing there. Fortunately Gus spoke German and within a half an hour he tracked her down, and was assured that her father had no need to worry about her condition.

One memorable visit to La Cruyeze was for a barbecue and a pig roasting. Gus and Lisa invited the three of us and some of our guests for this end of season event. Our guests had shown a keen interest in seeing for themselves how their hosts coped with living in isolation, and were curious about the farm, and of course were looking forward to eating some of the delicious pig meat. Spurred on by hunger and curiosity our guests climbed the steep path in failing light. I was concerned about our return because it would be pitch black by the time we returned, and our solitary torch would be in great demand.

The event was a great success, and our guests were treated to a tour of the ancient buildings and pig sties, and socialised with the crowd of guests who milled around the spit, hoping the meat would be cooked in time before they had to leave. However, by the time we had tasted the succulent meat it was time to grope our way towards the pathway, when we were interrupted by the snorting of wild boars that had gathered very close to the exit gate, blocking our way home in the pitch black night with these frightening creatures trampling the ground. Slowly we felt our way down towards our car with my torch, which was little more powerful than a Toc-H-lamp. We were relieved to reach Le Mas Pradel safely, and our visit provided our guests with lots to talk about during the remainder of their stay with us.

Andre and Christine

Most people would agree that good friends are often few and far between, especially when they move to an entirely different country, so it came as a very pleasant surprise that we became firm friends with Andre and Christine. He was an English teacher in France and his Scottish wife shared his love of Scottish dancing when he taught French in Edinburgh. Faye jumped at the opportunity to attend the English Circle Scottish dancing evening in our nearest town.

Faye told Christine that I would like to dance, with her knowing that I had little sense of timing. My embarrassment at the hash I made of the dance, which we were supposed to demonstrate, did at least amuse the French members, who tried to fathom out what I was doing trying to knot my legs out of time.

The next event was a Scotch tasting evening organised by Christine, who had collected lots of samples donated by well-known distillers. By the time the members had sampled every brand they had forgotten what it was like being sober.

Later on we were invited to our friends' town house, which had been constructed in stone and other expensive materials at vast expense, so it came as a surprise that they used an old deux chevaux for most of their local journeys, and kept their large shooting brake for high days and holidays. Andre explained that his runabout was ideal, because there was no road tax, it used hardly any fuel and it didn't worry him if the bad parkers damaged it.

Our friends enjoyed many an English Circle party which we hosted at the Mas, because it was an ideal venue for a large group, with room for dancing, relaxing in the salon, playing music in our library, floodlights for the boules games, or joining the pack in our very popular kitchen for refreshments.

Each Christmas we invited our friends who were alone to join us for the Christmas Day celebration. Andre and Christine's daughter was studying abroad, and their son was a chef so he was working elsewhere. Everybody thoroughly enjoyed themselves and we appreciated the way our friends helped with the preparations, clearing up, washing up, and contributing good wine and some of the food. The most valuable contribution was their cheerful company and good humour.

One hot summer evening we had been invited to our friends for a meal, prepared and cooked by their son who was a professional chef. However, the heat, lack of oxygen, good food and wine, together with smoking too many cigarettes, caused me to have an attack of asthma and a minor heart attack. Andre and Christine drove me to a doctor who refused to treat me because I wasn't one of his patients. They then took the three of us home where Faye took care of me and I recovered quite quickly.

Andre was convinced that the problem was caused by my smoking, and he was so upset by my attack that he forbade me from smoking ever again in his home. In retrospect Faye, our doctor and Andre were responsible for me giving up smoking. I owe them all a debt of gratitude for their help in breaking the habit, which prolonged my life by many years.

Unfortunately our friends moved to the other side of the Rhone, close to Mont Ventoux, where his family came from and owned lots of property and land. For many years the grandmother had lived with our friends, and it was hard going because she took a dislike to a Scottish lass marrying Andre. However, she died, leaving her son to inherit properties, vineyards and lots of agricultural land.

Two years after we had settled in back in the UK we spent our summer holiday visiting Saint Ambroix, and catching up with our many friends. We decided to cross the Rhone and spend some time in Orange visiting the Roman theatre, a museum and a gallery which had some interesting paintings by the Impressionists. We then booked into an hotel for the night and called at our friend's new home which was being renovated. Unfortunately nobody was at home, and one of the builders took us to be undesirables, and refused to let us wait indoors or stay on the property in case we were casing the joint. Fortunately Christine returned home just in time for us to be saved from being evicted by the burly builder.

Our reunion with our friends was very heartwarming and they were disappointed that we had arranged to stay elsewhere, but they insisted that we should join them for a slap-up meal in town, so that we could catch up with our changes in our lifestyle, without Alan. Lots of changes had occurred since we had last met. The old farmhouse which the three of us visited had been rented and they had moved into a larger and more prestigious property just down the road. They had acquired their new home, together with a substantial amount of desirable land, in a rather strange manner, because someone had already agreed to purchase the property. However, French law dictates that a farmer has the right to purchase land adjacent to his own providing an additional ten per cent of the agreed price is paid. The snag was that Andre was still teaching, and was unable to claim that he was a registered full-time farmer. At the last moment Christine agreed to become the registered farmer, so Andre was able to purchase all the land and properties on it. He became the sole owner of all the land and properties in their small community.

Their new home was being completely renovated at vast cost, and was going to be a superb residence, although they had to camp out in their caravan during the winter building works. Christine opened a door in her new kitchen and there it was looking more like a child's toy in the enormous room.

My favourite recollection of my friends was being invited to help them by picking grapes in one of their vineyards, which was not established for harvesting by mechanical means. It takes three days working hard for the pickers to cure their backache, as I found out when I tried to keep up with locals, who made it look so easy bending and turning their bodies in order to cut the bunches without damaging the grapes. The good nature of the pickers made the day's work more like a day out basking in the sun.

Christine left the vines before midday in order to cook a substantial meal for everybody to eat in the enormous kitchen, and of course drinking the previous year's red wine. During the afternoon Andre invited me to hitch a lift on his tractor to the vinery, to see how the grapes were weighed and how their alcohol content was measured. Providing the grapes were in good condition, the higher percentage of alcohol, the more he was paid for his crop. We then visited the large vineyards, which were being harvested by machines. This area is at a very high altitude and the grapes are always the last to be picked in France. Nearby Mont Ventoux dominates the surroundings, and is visible from Saint Ambroix.

One winter I saw the six thousand foot mountain coloured pink by the Sahara sand settling on the snow. At that time I had not been drinking the red wine from Andre's grapes. However, the wine from this region is one of my favourites, and each time I crack open a bottle of it I refresh my memories of happy days with my friends.

27

It's The All My Fault Club

During our season of letting the cottage and taking paying guests, our busy lives changed from building, renovating and gardening, to providing our guests with hospitality, cooking Continental and English food. Faye was our patron, chef, and general organiser. I was the waiter, housekeeper and gardener. Alan specialised in making chutney curry and preparing the desserts, and in his spare time repaired any mechanical or electrical items.

Considering that our combined ages totalled one hundred and eighty years when we first came to Saint Ambroix, our entire project of establishing a private hotel ran on well-oiled lines, largely due to Faye's personality and her hard work.

During the evening meals our guests often buttonholed me as I waited on table, with requests for information about tourist venues, sports activities and so on. This caused hold-ups in serving the different courses. Alan and Faye would hold a notice so that I could see into the kitchen, which told me to get a move on and not to slacken. If something went wrong in the kitchen or elsewhere, one or the other would shout out 'It's Richard's fault,' and over the months a light-hearted routine developed which blamed me for all the faults and problems of our establishment.

One evening a guest's wife commented that her husband, Eustace, always got things wrong, and she amused the other guests by recounting some of his mistakes, caused by his forgetfulness. He then told us that his wife called him Useless Eustace.

The thought crossed my mind that having someone in the household who was willing to accept the blame no matter whose fault it was would reduce any arguments. It would be an excellent idea to start a club called It's The All My Fault Club. Gradually my friends and some of our guests took to the idea, so I provided some ground rules for any future members.

I suggest that the idea could be developed in places of work, where the employers should pay the elected members of It's the All My Fault Club to rid the firm of back biting and arguments, as there would be no need to waste time apportioning blame. I am now considering setting up a website as my contribution to National Harmony. Long-service members would of course be entitled to wear the ornamental regalia which would be presented by myself, the Founder and President of ITAMFC.

28

Antiques and Sales

Prior to our lives in France, Alan and Faye had been very professional in their dealings of pieces of antique furniture and bric-a-brac. They were well known in the auction houses in Plymouth as 'Greene with three e's'. By the time we left England we had loaded Pickfords' largest continental pantechnicon with some fine antique items of furniture and a collection of their son's paintings, together with appropriate items of furniture and furnishings from our three houses.

Some antiques

BONNE CHANCE

The staircase

The highest ceiling

It wasn't until Pickfords had emptied the contents of the pantechnicon into the Mas that we realised we would have to scour the area for extra suitable items of furniture and furnishings, to fill the empty spaces, with items which would be in keeping with the period of our home.

The first house sale we attended was an old Mas on the outskirts of our town. It was packed with eager buyers, so we had little time to view the lots. The first item we needed was a round antique table, large enough to seat six. The next item was a Napoleon mirror which I fell in love with. I was successful with both my bids, much to the annoyance of several dealers.

Our first visit to an auction house was in the Cevennes a long way from St Ambroix. However, it turned out to be disappointing with only two paintings which Alan spotted, and said that they were both large enough for our salon, and were interesting. The first one was a religious painting mounted in an outstanding elliptical frame, which was quite valuable in itself. The second painting was of the Devil watching maidens dancing in a clearing in the woods. Both paintings were up for sale in the same lot. Alan bid £20 worth of francs for them, but was thunderstruck to be presented with a strange feather bedspread instead. He was so enraged, he shouted that he had been swindled and he insisted he had the paintings instead. The auctioneer agreed, but we wondered if he was fixing the lot in favour of one of the dealers who was expecting to get the paintings on the cheap. These fascinating works of art have often been admired.

Another auction house closer to the Mas proved to be equally filled with tat, although I purchased a Louis Phillipe chair at what I thought to be a bargain piece. Unfortunately I found worm and damage to one of the rear legs, which I managed to repair and make another carved leg in its place. Several years later I sold it at a car boot sale for a very good price to a dealer, who thought he had a bargain. A year or more later I happened to see him at the same car boot sale, and he wasn't at all pleased when he found that his chair had been repaired. He said that another time he would take care to check that his bargains were worthwhile. It is a mistake that buyers are all too often carried away with the first impression they have, without appraising lots very carefully.

Faye had a very good eye for a bargain, and spotted a very good working kitchen table, which she thought could be modified to be used as a refectory table for our dining room, instead of our round one. The shopkeeper agreed to exchange his for ours, thinking that he had the better bargain. However, it was a simple job to reduce the width of the top rails so that diners could get their legs comfortably under the table top, and with a lot of elbow grease, or rather beeswax, we had the perfect table for a very modest price, which was only half the cost a similar genuine antique one.

Rummaging around recycling depots, antique and bric-a-brac shops, and scouring adverts in the local papers for anything we needed, was Alan and Faye's favourite pastime. A firm which specialised in bankrupt stock provided us with a double porcelain sink unit, and a delightful Italian chandelier for our salon, for a fraction of their value.

The recycling depot sold us a glazed and panelled door which we used to replace the old dining room door, which would have looked more at home in a cattle shed. The foyer looked quite elegant with the new door as it provided some extra light, and it looked as though it had been crafted specially for its purpose. At the time I was not enthusiastic about collecting it from the depot as I was in the middle of a major job of constructing a stone wall to support the huge vaulted ceilings in the master bedroom and the dining room. Alan and Faye eventually persuaded me to down tools, fit the car roof rack and collect their precious find. What a difference it made to the impression our guests had as they entered our front door, and it was well worth me taking time out to install it.

After I had built the stone wall, all that it needed was something outstanding to put in the niche. An advert in our local paper sent us scurrying into Alès where a house sale was about to start and we were anxious not to miss any bargains. On our arrival at the small terraced house, which had been owned by Russian émigrés, we had a job to elbow our way in, because of the press of buyers all trying to find something worthwhile. I managed to rummage through the stacks of books which were hardly going to be purchased as they were all in Russian. It was just as well because I spotted a dirty-looking bust of a young maiden hidden behind a pile of long-playing records of Russian music and some antiquated kitchen appliances. I didn't have long to wait for the auctioneer to wade through the lots with the speed of a TGV. He was so bored with trying to sell the unwanted junk that he knocked the young maiden down to me for only a hundred francs. Brian, Faye's artist son, cleaned and painted the bust, which remained contented in her niche in the stone wall for the rest of our time in the Mas.

When Yoko's wife eventually died in our local hospice, his son decided that the safest place for his father would be to move him to the USA where he would be cared for in a special village for OAPs like himself, and close enough to his son, Antonni. He was given power of attorney to deal with the sale of the family home and the contents. Faye was instrumental in helping to conclude the sale of the house, and Antonni negotiated the sale of the valuable antiques to a reliable dealer. He offered the three of us to take our pick of the remaining items at very generous prices, in light of the years the three of us had helped his mother and father through their traumas.

While Faye and I were clearing out the junk, the household clearance men tried to purloin several items we had bought. I caught the boss carrying away my statuette in his arms. When I remonstrated with him he became furious at the lost opportunity to make off with my treasure. He deliberately decapitated the statuette, hoping that I was going to let him have it thinking it was beyond repair. Fortunately I was able to repair the fine soapstone statuette, and with some careful carving nobody could tell that it had ever been damaged.

Faye asked if there were any mirrors she could have, and I willingly paid for some fine antique ones, which enhanced our old Mas. The finest of all was a beautiful brass mirror which had never been taken out of its original packing. Her treasure has been admired by dealers, and a specialist from one of London's most prestigious auction houses.

During Antonni's problems with his father's irrational behaviour and his mother's illness, the three of us adopted him as our own. The Mas was a fitting place to display some of Antonni's family mementos, and he always made himself at home.

On his first visit to the Mas after his father had been settled in his new care home, Antonni arrived with his new wife, who sported Doc Martin boots, and worked as an engineer. She most likely was far more enthusiastic about hockey than sex, so we didn't rate their marriage would last. Divorce was inevitable and his next girlfriend soon took him to meet her family who lived in the hills and farmed for a living.

The mother insisted that Antonni shared a meal of grits with the family. This seemed to signify that this was the custom when the couple were engaged. He had the sense not to have hillbillies as his in-laws. Several years later he found his soulmate, who was a Russian art agent, a sensitive loving partner who brought happiness to his life, after the trials and tribulations he had endured for so many years.

29

Storm Clouds

Our rose-coloured horizons began to be menaced by ill health and approaching old age. Jack Bazalgette and his family had joined the three of us, together with several friends who were at a loss for company during Christmas Day. It came as a shock to see Jack's health had seriously deteriorated and he needed to spend the best part of Christmas afternoon in the bedroom adjacent to the dining room. Naturally our concerns for his health cast a shadow on the festive season, and it was a sharp reminder that we were all heading towards our final retirement. Nevertheless we enjoyed ourselves and Jack managed to tuck in to the traditional luncheon.

Not long after the New Year we heard that our friend had been admitted into hospital and was rapidly losing his memory, but much to his wife's surprise he recognised Faye and he even managed to crack a joke when we visited him. His demise was particularly sad because he left behind a grieving widow who had lived life to the full with her husband, who was to be sadly missed by countless friends, and those whom he had helped.

John, our humorist friend, advised us to consider returning to the UK before ill health caught up with us or we found ourselves unable to maintain our large property, or unable to take in guests, which had provided us with enough extra income to keep our finances afloat. For my part I optimistically chose to weather the storm if it headed in our direction.

The storm struck without any forewarning, when Alan told Faye he feared that he had cancer. Nurse Faye immediately accompanied Alan to consult Dr Gorgas about his problem. A single telephone call to a specialist arranged a consultation the following day. The diagnosis confirmed our worst fears. Our storm cloud burst with a violence which was to be a life-changing event.

However Alan was determined to go ahead with the holiday we had booked in Nice, as he had invited Judy his sister to share our apartment close to the harbour and we had all been looking forward to another super holiday in my favourite venue. Faye gave Alan his anti-cancer injections every day, and he never complained about his illness during the holiday. Instead he was determined to enjoy every minute, even when we had to buy waterproof capes because of the monsoon downpours, and the hilly roads which became cascades, pressure hosing everything in sight.

We returned home after our four-star holiday, to face up to the reality of giving up our business and changing our dining room into a single ward where Faye could nurse Alan. Eventually he was admitted into the teaching hospital at Nimes for tests and treatment. Every day without fail we drove to Nimes and remained by his bedside as long as possible, because he desperately needed our company. We returned home exhausted, hungry and full of hope that his treatment would improve his condition.

Alan was given permission to return home for Christmas, because he was desperate to spend the time with us in the Mas, and I believe he wished to remain with us for the remainder of his life. Some days afterwards Dr Gorgas told us that there was nothing more he could do for Alan, and he prescribed enough morphine to keep his pain at bay.

Alan told Faye that he hoped that she and I would share a home together if we returned to the UK, but at this stage it was our last priority to make plans, especially as we had been so happy together. Alan had made a monumental effort to keep his spirits up until his last day.

Our neighbours and close friends rallied round us when Alan died, and they carried him out of the house to the hearse, as the local custom dictates. The following morning our police chief and neighbour burst into tears when we told him the bad news. Everyone including Jasper and Katie helped us cope with the loss of our dear friend.

The English Circle Members, our friends and relations swelled the congregation in the chapel of the crematorium to capacity. However,

STORM CLOUDS

the service was delayed because the equipment broke down, and we had to wait for ages before it was repaired. Alan was noted for carrying a small toolkit wherever he went, and he was always mending things which had broken.

Faye gave me a nudge after we had been twiddling our fingers with no prospect of the service starting. She said that she expected Alan to open the coffin and say, 'Step aside I'll mend the damn thing myself.'

Alan had been in his element living in the Mas, where he had an Aladdin's Cave with all the tools he needed. In every other respect our way of life fulfilled his needs, and we were very grateful for the happy years we had spent among such good folk.

Mai telephoned Faye from London, to say that she had a premonition of Alan's death, and mentioned the time he had 'visited her'. There was no possible way that she could have received the news by any conventional means.

30

Our Future

The decision to face up to the prospect of having to relocate and downsize, because Faye and I had insufficient incomes to support our current lifestyle, made the choice of our options concerning where we lived very difficult. We had loved living in St Ambroix in such a super property, with such good neighbours and town folk.

However, the more we compared the reality of remaining in France with relocating to Billericay, the more we realised that John's advice was the most sensible, although it was the least desirable.

Our friend Mai was also considering her own position, which was even more problematic than our own. She offered us a generous alternative of living with her in the Mazel, which boasted a private

Mai Zetterling and the author, 1993

theatre with its marble floor and balcony. The view from the impressive stone-built covered terrace, across Mai's own valley where she had her own organic allotment, was breathtaking on a clear day, when Mont Blanc could be seen. Mai's offer was very inviting, but we declined it despite having such happy memories of her, and the Mazel.

The die was cast, and we made plans to purchase a property where Alan and Faye's family lived. It was however very difficult to overcome all the numerous obstacles before we managed to complete our move.

The process of selling a property in France is complicated and very expensive, because the Notaires collect the taxes which are due when a property owner dies, and they have to wind up the estate, which is also expensive and time consuming.

The Napoleonic Laws were introduce to ensure that the working classes could own land and property, and to this end property is kept within the family, and is proportioned depending on the number of inheritors. A widow like Faye only received a third of Alan's estate, as both her sons did, but the entire cost of settling the taxes, and the Notaire's costs, were deducted from Faye's share, leaving her with much less than her sons.

These old laws are outdated in my opinion because they were activated when women were regarded as being of less importance, and were discriminated against when their husbands died, all in the cause of keeping the property within the family. One of our English Circle members inherited a twenty-eighth share of an established farm, but unfortunately the inheritors could not agree to the sale of the farm, and some of the less wealthy ones could not raise their contribution towards maintaining the buildings and the land. Consequently the place went to rack and ruin, and the land and buildings taxes were left unpaid for years. The commune was within its rights to take possession of the farm, providing it was to benefit the tax-paying residents. These windfall possessions sometimes raised so much money that the local taxes could be slashed.

Some excellent advice for prospective emigrants looking forward to saving money is to settle in one of these lucky communes, and they should keep a small property, even a single room will do. Providing they have a bona fide address in the UK, this will ensure that an English will will be accepted by the authorities, and this will save paying all the French taxes if someone dies when they are residing in France.

Having found a purchaser for the Mas, we were surprised to find that the German wife had the right to sleep in the house the night before taking possession. We did our best to make the new owners at home, but after the ten o'clock news the husband told me that his wife would not purchase, because the floor tiles under the large Indian carpet in the salon had not been painted. By chance I still had enough tile paint to complete the task some four hours later.

The following morning the Notaire duly completed the formalities of conveying the ownership of Le Mas Pradel, handed over the large door key and bade us good day. I was dumbfounded that we had not received a single franc, let alone nearly a million francs. Did the Notaire think that we were so stupid as to leave his office without an official document stating that we were owed the correct amount which was due to us? My reprimand produced the document without an apology, and in a bad temper.

It transpired that Notaires have the right to retain their clients' money for three weeks. But even after the three weeks were up, there were no signs that he was going to pay us our dues, as he was making a substantial interest on our 900,000 francs. However, we had the

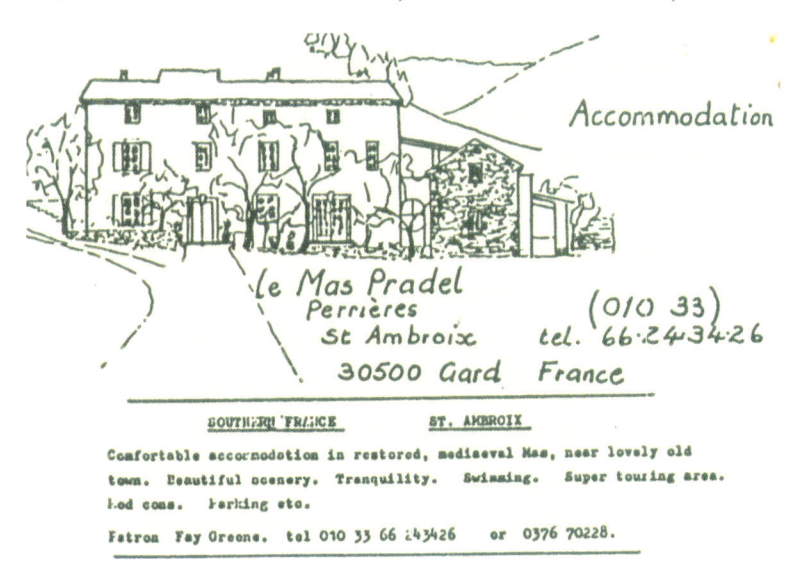

Accommodation

Le Mas Pradel
Perrières
St Ambroix   *tel. (010 33) 66·24·34·26*
30500 Gard   France

SOUTHERN FRANCE   ST. AMBROIX

Comfortable accomodation in restored, mediaeval Mas, near lovely old town. Beautiful scenery. Tranquility. Swimming. Super touring area. Mod cons. Parking etc.

Patron Fay Greene. tel 010 33 66 243426   or 0376 70228.

Le Fin

good fortune to know that one of the English Circle members' brother was a senior executive in a major Scottish bank. His sister asked him to advise us what we could do, as we were unable to finalise the purchase of our Billericay house because we hadn't received our cash. We had been living hand to mouth in a variety of accommodation, with a kind neighbour who had stored our belongings in her empty garage.

Our Scottish Good Samaritan asked his Paris colleagues to look into the matter on our behalf, and their prompting succeeded in getting our blood out of the Notaire's stone.

A few months after we had settled into our new home, we learnt that our dear friend Mai Zetterling had been staying in a friend's apartment in London while she was receiving treatment for cancer. A week or two later she phoned us and asked us to visit her in the Edward VII Hospital for Officers. The very next day we travelled up to town with heavy hearts and some flowers. We were vetted before we were taken to a sumptuous single ward which was fit for royalty, in fact each of the single wards on the first floor is named after a member of the Royal family, who had been patients there.

Our reunion with Mai was observed by Matron, who said that the door was to be kept open. Mai said, 'Close the damn door Faye, I think the old boot has gone.' For our entire visit Mai let her hair down, and laughter, and memories of our years of friendship, put our sadness on the back burner until we departed. It was only too apparent that our dear friend had made her last live performance.